HAITI,

CRUEL AND UNUSUAL PUNISHMENT

GERARD GERMAIN, MD

ISBN: 979-8-89419-227-7 (sc)
ISBN: 979-8-89419-228-4 (hc)
ISBN: 979-8-89419-229-1 (e)

Because of the dynamic nature of the Internet, any web addresses or links contained in this book may have changed since publication and may no longer be valid. The views expressed in this work are solely those of the author and do not necessarily reflect the views of the publisher, and the publisher hereby disclaims any responsibility for them.

THE EWINGS
PUBLISHING

One Galleria Blvd., Suite 1900, Metairie, LA 70001
(504) 702-6708

Special thanks to:

Honorable Ambassador Alcid Raymond Joseph editor of "Haiti Observateur" and Former Haitian Ambassador to the United States in Washington DC.

Dr. Fayette the anchor of Haiti Premiere class.

Mr. Wendell Theodore of Radio Tele Metropole LE POINT, a Haitian Media Personality.

Without whom this book would not have been possible

Of all my 20 years of giving a single dollar coin to people, I have never met someone ever, even a millionaire, who refused to take it. These IKE dollars are amazing. It is not much but changes the tone of any conversation. It makes people happy. And… people never forget the gesture. Here is your IKE dollar.

THE IKE DOLLAR

The proceed of this book will go to the construction of the Gerard Isly Germain Elementary School.

CONTENTS

FOREWORD

In Gerald Germain's book "Haiti, cruel and unusual punishment", readers are taken on a thought-provoking journey that delves deep into the complexities of Haiti's history, politics, and socio-economic landscape. Germain's ability to ask compelling questions that challenge the reader's understanding of the situation in Haiti is truly commendable. His analysis connects the dots between various factors such as politics, history, and economics, shedding light on the motivations behind the actions of both the Haitian people and external forces influencing the country.

One of the standout features of Germain's work is his unapologetic examination of the world's hypocrisy towards Haiti and its people. Through a humanitarian lens, he exposes the harsh realities faced by Haiti and critiques the actions of those who claim to have the country's best interests at heart. By offering solutions and drawing parallels with other nations like El Salvador that have overcome similar challenges, Germain presents a glimmer of hope for Haiti's future.

While the content of the book may be difficult to digest due to its unfiltered portrayal of Haiti's struggles, Germain's honest approach paves the way for constructive dialogue and the possibility of positive change. By emphasizing the importance of Haitians taking charge of their own destiny and advocating for social justice, Germain empowers readers to confront uncomfortable truths and work towards a brighter future for their country.

In conclusion, " Haiti, cruel and unusual punishment " by Gerard Germain is a powerful and eye-opening read that challenges readers to confront the harsh realities of Haiti's past and present. By offering insightful analysis and practical solutions, Germain inspires hope and calls for action from those who have the courage to stand up for social justice. This book is a must-read for anyone seeking a deeper understanding of Haiti's challenges and a roadmap towards a better tomorrow. Thank you, Gerard Germain, for your courageous voice and invaluable contribution to the discourse on Haiti's future.

—Pei Desrosiers

INTRODUCTION

The biggest problem with the insecurity spreading in Haiti is the inability of the leadership of the country to see or recognize urgency. I work in an emergency room, and I can tell you, if a nurse or a doctor doesn't see a problem when it emerges, it might be tackled too late. That is exactly what is happening in Haiti. It's taking so long for them to decide. It is taking too long for them to administer the remedy, while people are dying at an alarming rate. They do not take into account that the medication takes a while to be effective. By the time they're done, they are going to leave the place in a vacuum, as was done a few years back after the exit of the MINUSTAH, the United Nations Stabilization Mission in Haiti. Soon in the future we will go back to the same problem again. There's a new generation that is presently learning how to commit crimes by observing the heavily armed bandits. Why can't we learn from our mistakes? Justice too long delayed is justice denied.

It is well known by all that Haiti is in trouble, to say the least. The president has been assassinated. There's no executive, no judicial, no legislative, no prime minister, no army, no navy. Neighboring countries are deeply involved in Haiti's affairs. There is no transportation to or communication with the outside world, no air transport, no commercial airlines. The streets are barricaded. Crossing the barricades is guaranteed suicide. While all this is happening, the country is dependent on the outside world for food, because all our plantations have been destroyed in a multi-year coordinated effort. The army was disbanded by order of the United States, the United Nations (UN), or both, at the behest of former President Jean-Bertrand Aristide. The country is now run by a multitude of gangs all over the country, but concentrated mostly in and around the capital, Port-au-Prince, 80% of which is under gang control, according to a U.N. report.

It is within your right not to read this short history lesson about Haiti. It is within your right to ignore the genocide in Haiti. However, you have no right to comment about something that you have not read about or of which you have no knowledge. Remember that when basic human rights are denied to one, they are denied to all. As far as I am concerned, I am certain that the way human rights are perceived in the developed countries cannot apply to Haiti. It will need to be gradual and cannot be done without the education of the nation. It is unbelievable that the population can be suffering so much and that such turmoil is occurring next to a land of plenty. While I believe that many Haitians in Haiti are undercover criminals, for keeping silent when the action of the criminals helps them financially, Haitians, in general, wherever they're living, must be considered as victims. Haitians are futureless, and Haiti is doomed to remain a failed state.

Monique le chic

CHAPTER 1

SEQUENCE OF EVENTS

HOW DID WE GET THERE?

Granted, what is happening did not start yesterday or today. Haitians have always been the forgotten people of the world. But, if Haitians did not sell their country, no one would have been able to buy it.

Jean Claude Duvalier, nicknamed Baby Doc, got married. His father-in-law became very powerful. He never had enough. The rumor was that every business had to give him a cut. He was running the business part of the country. People began to get upset and that led, in 1986, to the overthrow of Baby Doc, nicknamed who took over after the father, François "Papa Doc," Duvalier died in 1971. In the early nineteen eighties, when Baby Doc was toppled, the country was experiencing the highest GDP ever, the economy gaining around 5% annually. It was too good to be true. When the country was about to get out of the hole, turbulence started. Was it coincidental?

Some international organizations that already were putting pressure on young Duvalier, such as the International Monetary Fund (IMF), and the World Bank, all headed by France, finally put their grip on Haiti and imposed the policy of privatization. In the process, a lot of industries have gone under, stolen on paper, or sold to other countries.

The process was an indescribable looting. The Dominican Republic being the primary beneficiary.

The GDP started plunging. The *gourde,* the national currency, which had been linked to the U.S. dollar since 1919, at the rate of 5 *gourdes* to one dollar ($ 1), was unlinked.

The banditry of our times in Haiti began when Rudolph Giuliani was mayor of New York City and President Bill Clinton was in the White House. To reduce crime in the city and, at the same time save money, the prisoners who finished serving their sentence in New York were repatriated. Thus, many Haitians—and non-Haitians also,—who had never been in Haiti or even spoke the language, were sent (supposedly back) to Haiti. Just as I said in the **GGTLM** book (short for "**Gérard Germain, The Luckiest Man Who Grew-UP In An Engineered and Manufactured Poverty**"), what people have been accustomed to do in their first 25 years of life, they tend to continue doing in their remaining 75 years, if they make it that long. These "repatriated" guys were up to no good. They have been accustomed to committing crimes during their first quarter of life on earth. Obviously, no change will suddenly occur, they must practice what they've preached through action, for they have mastered their art, which is crime.

Then came the inauguration of President Jean-Bertrand Aristide. To stay in power, after he had encouraged the massacre of some *"Tontons Macoute,"* the official thugs of the Duvalier regime, the priest-turned-president openly said that he likes the smell of *"Père Lebrun,"* the used car tires that were sold by a Port-au-Prince merchant of that name, usually in the slums of Cité Soleil in the capital. The smell of Père Lebrun means that of the tire around the neck of someone being burned alive. Can you imagine that the mixture of tire and flesh burning sending the priest-president into a trance! No trial, no jury for the victim, just an accusation leading to a crude execution! President Aristide also started his various units of the *Chimères,* (Ghosts), under such names as the

"Sadham Hussein Army," the "Little Machetes Army," the "Sleep in the Woods Army," even the "Cannibal Army" and more. These groups carried out his orders, often as their leader was persuasively speaking publicly. They were accused of committing many crimes in the country. That even continued, following the leader's exile. The purpose of the *Chimères.* while not stated, was no different from that of the Duvalier goons that President Aristide was trying to eradicate. He had formed his own militia, just like the *Tontons-Macoute* thugs that they replaced. President Aristide was also accused of forming a special unit in the *Cité Soleil* slum called *"Rat pa kaka"* (No Shitting Rats), a group composed mostly of underaged children who were armed to the teeth. I am not a fan of Aristide, but the mere fact that he was removed from power in Haiti is an indication that he was up to something good, besides all the wrongs.

The army was disbanded, and some of the soldiers were arrested and handcuffed by elements of the United States Army, of course with President Aristide's approval.

By JAMES CESAR WAH
HAITIAN ARMY ARREST BY THE US ARMY

Can someone convince me that closing the army of a country could not lead to insecurity? If you are unable to convince me, can I safely say that when the army was dismantled, it was known already and maybe planned already that the insecurity was coming. To be fair, I performed and inquisition on the web about the role of an army to see if destroying the army was a good idea. The first definition of the army is to maintain the security of a country. It was then known from the beginning that no army would negatively affect Haiti. Not having an army, the biggest employer of the country also affected the economy by decreasing the flow of money in the general population. Even if the Haitian population had asked to close the army, didn't the United Nations and the United States of America know that it was going to cause this calamity? Why was it done? Was it part of the general plan for Haiti?

For their own protection and in a move to amass more power, some powerful politicians resorted to forming their own army by paying uneducated and unscrupulous individuals, who had no real future, just to commit illegal acts for them. The situation degenerated and the armed groups started a lucrative kidnapping business, which has known no bounds. Victims of kidnaping were at all levels of society.

Business was so good that the gangs regrouped and started blocking the streets, demanding that toll be paid, to allow passage to drivers of vehicles. With the collected funds the gangs had what was needed to purchase imported drugs from countries like Colombia and become drug exporters to the United States, further north and elsewhere, and at the same time importers of all sorts of weapons Made in the USA

The situation got out of control. The bandits were making the laws, though unwritten. They became masters of the night. If you happen to be sick, you had better stay home. For, it's more certain that you'll be killed in the streets than by the disease from which you're suffering, no matter who you are. At one point it was said that the Prime Minister wanted to visit Cap-Haitian, the second city of the country. To do so, he had to bribe the bandits to let him pass. If he could bribe them, then he knew who they were. Regarding moving about in the country, there has been a curfew without any official order. In some areas of the land, your mandatory alarm clock is the sound of the AR15 being used to execute someone outside your door, with the smell of that person's burning flesh jolting you. Hopefully, he was dead before being burned. In times like that, you only close your eyes, remain silent and pray, even if you don't believe in God.

Then, the President of the Republic was assassinated in the bedroom of his highly secured home, in an upscale neighborhood. Reportedly, several Colombian mercenaries, pretending to be DEA agents, entered the compound, undeterred by the presidential guard, and penetrated the residence and entered the bedroom, shooting the president a dozen times. None of the president's protectors shot a bullet, nor suffered a scratch. I will not ask why the simple word DEA was powerful enough to freeze the president's guards, who put down their arms.

Two main jails in the country, one in the capital and the other in a suburb, were broken into and thousands of prisoners, including some gang members and the Colombian killers, who were incarcerated in them, were liberated. Was that part of a plan for the jailbreaks?

Anyway, there have been all sorts of speculations regarding the assassination and investigations supposedly have been undertaken in Haiti and elsewhere, including in the United States. Three years have passed, and there has been "No Justice for the President," as a slogan called for. And one wonders why a federal judge in Florida in charge of the dossier of the president's assassination, has granted the U.S. prosecutors their request by sealing some of the evidence concerning the assassination, under the pretext of "National Security!" Wasn't that done also in the case of President John Fitzgerald Kennedy, assassinated in broad daylight, in Dallas, Texas, on November 22, 1963?

Every single one of these events represented one more nail used in the construction of Haiti's coffin.

Back to the scene in Port-au-Prince. If there are shootings in the street in the morning you dare not go out in search of food. Your only option is to stay home that day with an empty stomach. At least you'll still have your life. Even a president cannot get a semblance of justice! In that case, one just manages to find a safe corner to stay, hoping to see the next day.

Haiti has been a crime on steroid, since the president's assassination on July 7, 2021.

While people were dying of starvation and of senseless killing everywhere, especially in the capital, debates were going on at the United Nations. The USA was debating. They had other more pressing problems to which to attend. They finally agreed that 1,000 Kenyan police officers would be sent to Haiti, but for months they took their time waiting to act. I will not mention the Prime Minister here, because he was never present. He never even acknowledged the deliberate burning down of multiple neighborhoods by the bandits in the capital, acting as if nothing had happened. Maybe he was absent when that happened. For a neurosurgeon not to have a sense of compassion is unimaginable! Meanwhile people are dying at an alarming rate. One can't keep up with the body count.

CHAPTER 2

HOW CAN IT BE JUST MISFORTUNE?

The final draw: Haiti has been trashed by delinquency.

The ultimate order is and has always been to destroy Haiti entirely and make it hell-on-earth. I said so in **GGTLM,** in 2019. Haiti was lucky that it has not disappeared yet from the surface of the earth. But in a way, I was wrong. Haiti has disappeared. If you did not realize that, it's just your blindness. Job well done.

Here is my list of Haitian misfortunes:

Generally, in life there are ups and downs. In Haiti's situation, however, the chart has been straight down. It is so striking that the slope gets steeper as the days pass. The next bad news is always worse than the previous one. The bad news is continuous and there is no good news on the horizon. Here are some bad news to help you understand.

-2016 the one time that Haiti was able to afford the Miss Universe Paget, Raquel Pelisier, Haitian was one of the last competitors standing. She was now competing with France. France won the Paget. She did not have to get that far. Haitians would have been happy that she just participated. Loosing to France however was a disaster. This is so typical in the history of Haiti. We had to compete with France and lose. What is the odd of that happening? Was that a message? Was that a lesson again? It feels like some force is helping nature decide on Haiti.

-The factual Indemnity. Well, explained in chapters 12 and 13 in this book.

-The creation of *"Banque Nationale d'Haïti,"* imposed by France, to extort money from the country. In a series that ran in May 2022, the New York Times reported that some investors in France were collecting 35% interest on their investments in Haiti, while the Haitian government could not even borrow money from their own bank. That is what I called *"Poignard"* (Dagger) in the book ***"Eiffel Tower, Pride of Haiti"***

By ISMAEL ST. LOUIS
HAITI CARRYING FRANCE ON ITS BACK FOR CENTURIES.

-The plotting to constantly overthrow Haitian presidents. (In the history of Haiti, all the presidents have either been killed or overthrown, except for the Haitian presidents during some kind of American Occupation. (A Haitian president that has remained in power for his whole term was either no good for the country or was in cahoots with a foreign power. A vivid example is Prime Minister Ariel Henry who stayed in power for 3 years and accomplished nothing.

-The claim that Haitians were the cause of HIV infection, or AIDS. Being Haitian, initially in 1982, one was designated to be among the risk factor groups for AIDS. An extremely damaging assumption to the image of Haiti and its associated consequences. The 4-H Club, blamed for the vectors of the disease, stood for Haitians, Homosexuals, Hemophiliacs and Heroin addicts. In 1983, the CDC and the FDA, dubbed Federal Discrimination Administration by Haitians, used their 4-H Club theory to explain the risks to AIDS in America. It turned out that being Haitian had nothing to do with it. And on April 20, 1990, thousands of Haitians, reportedly close to 1000,000, marched from Brooklyn to downtown Manhattan making the Brooklyn Bridge tremble, forcing the CDC and the FDA to back down and drop the Haitian name from their 4-H Club. The damage, however, was already done.

-There's the claim that leather from Haiti was infected with anthrax. That had the purpose of destroying the lucrative business of mats and rugs made of leather that Haiti was exporting, especially to the United States.

By CESAR WAH
"COCHON NOIR", HAITI'S INDIGENOUS PORK,
SACRIFISED BECAUSE OF SWINE FLU.

-There's the plague of the *Cochon noir,* or Haitian black pig, that resembles the boar, that thrived no matter the diet. All of them were slaughtered in 1978, under the pretext of being responsible for Asian swine flu. Now, we depend on imported pork food from the United States of America. Meanwhile, the white pig introduced in Haiti never adapted. Neither was it of any help in the general cleanup by eating the garbage that the black pig used to eat. I am not even going to mention that the black pig was like money in the bank for the peasants and also was prominent in voodoo ceremonies. Without the black pig, some ceremonies are impossible. Also, the imported pork from the USA doesn't have the same taste as that of the indigenous pig.

-The hard, fleshy Haitian chicken also disappeared.

-Lemon and lime trees are drying up, despite irrigation.

-The eradication of cocoa, coffee and sugar cane plantations, to be replaced with plantations of rubber trees by SHADA, a so-called joint venture between the United States of America and Haiti, to expand wartime production of rubber in Haiti's countryside. The rubber trees never produced any fruit, whereas these plants were supposed to boost the economy of Haiti. That never happened.

-The same thing was orchestrated for the plantation of Vetiver and Sisal (pitre) in Haiti.

-The coconut trees are disappearing, drying up or desiccating. It looks as if Haiti is being starved.

-The extraction of bauxite and the promise that pines would be planted to disguise the craters made was never carried out by the Reynolds Company in Miragoâne, in the Nippes region.

-The Sedren Company was extracting copper in Gonaives, and reading American books, Haitians will discover that Sedren was exporting gold also, without the knowledge of the government.

-Some important part of our folklore has been stolen. Tourists love what they see and hear in Haiti. When they return to their respective countries, they take possession of certain items as if it's theirs. Take the song *"Ti zwazo"* with the refrain *"Choucoune se te youn Marabou,"* it's an example of such a phenomenon.

-The name *"Madame Gougousse"* for a rice of Haitian origin is no longer Haitian. It is sold mostly in Haitian neighborhoods in the diaspora, but it is imported from Southeast Asia. How did they apprehend the name is unknown to me. Was that part of the plan to destroy Haitian rice plantations?

-*Pèpè* or *Kennedy,* as second-hand clothing and hand-me-down, cheap stuff from the United States sold in public markets or by vendors on sidewalks, destroyed the local manufacturing system of the Haitian clothing business.

-Even the mentality has been changing. I never could imagine a church having its own funeral parlor. With the inflow of money diminished in the churches, due to a decrease in membership, reflecting the expansion of insecurity which doesn't spare the houses of worship, some churches have opened adjoining Funeral Homes to increase their income,

-I have to say also that President Aristide with the establishment of the *"Chimères"* (Ghosts) contributed greatly to the destabiïlization and devastation of the country and its economy. The introduction of the *Chimères,* one could say, was the beginning of today's gangs, leading to the widespread problem of insecurity. When President Aristide, with international support, destroyed the Haitian army in January 1995, after returning from golden exile in Washington, on October 15. 1994, under the protection of 24,000 U.S. troops, he created a security vacuum that he attempted to fill with his *Chimères.*

And arm embargo imposed on the Haitian army is still in place. Moreover, a Police Force isnt't trained to fight heavily armed gangs. So, the Haitian National Police (French acronym PNH) has failed miserably in standing up to the gangs that have not failed in attacking its members, even taking over some Police precincts. There hasn't been any official lifting of the US embargo on weapons to Haiti's miniscule army remobilized under Jovenel Moïse, making it difficult for the government to fight the gangs. **Apparently, Haiti doesn't have the right to defend itself. Why?**

-The repatriation of criminals even if they were not born in the country or cannot speak the language is deleterious to the country. These repatriated individuals, as previously mentioned, were dumped in Haiti after they served their sentences in some jails that are some sorts of "criminal education centers" in the United States. Now, in Haiti, they are applying their vast knowledge of their trade, that of committing crime, which was learned in the US. Easily, they have made connection to the gun traffickers, themselves connected with some of their patrons among Haiti's oligarchy. There you have it, a gang culture grandly established.

Unfortunately, there is more: The United Nations came to Haiti, in 2004, with MINUSTAH, the United Nations for the Stability of Haiti. The Nepalese contingent introduced cholera in 2010, killing 10,000 by the end of 2019, and infecting several thousands more. Cholera, that was unknown in Haiti is now endemic. When the MINUSTHA troops left, 13 years later, the horny UN soldiers had left a slew of fatherless children, born either of rape or from the poor women who were paid a few dollars to give of themselves. The UN never admitted responsibility in such mayhem. And Haiti was left more unstable than before, with gangs having sprouted under the glare of the MINUSTHA.

-Prime Minister Gérard Latortue was a high cadre of the United Nations. His first move after his nomination to the post, in 2004, was to travel to France to declare that the claim of $21 billion in reparations from the former enslavers, that President Aristide had mentioned, is pure stupidity. As for me, I want to give credit to anyone that has tried to help Haiti. After a declaration like that of Latortue's, can one wonder whether he signed any document annulling the official claim of reparation from President Aristide. What else did he sign?

-The present Prime Minister of Haiti, Dr. Garry Conille, is aware of UN's modus operandi. He had a long career in the international organization. He is known by the top officials there and he knows them also. They've bumped into each other in the UN hallways. They attend the same parties. They have each other's special phone numbers. Could his nomination have been dictated by the UN? Is there any secret deal made? Could this nomination be a UN self-serving agenda?

According to widely published information, in 2010, then Secretary of State Hilary Clinton pushed to reverse the results of an election in Haiti to favor Michel Joseph Martelly. He did not even make the cut. He did not have any qualification to lead a country. No didactic, no vision for the country, no traditional character, no integrity based on what he has said in public. Except for his popularity from his music business. He was a cursing singer of a Haitian band. He is gross and vulgar. He even nicknamed himself the "Legal Bandit." Isn't that humiliating? Do I need to enumerate anymore? Nonetheless, I will give him some credit. When time came for him to leave the scene, he left, period. Granted he had organized a "selection" to put the "Banana Man" in office to warm the couch for him. And now, after all the scandals surrounding the heist of some $4 billion from the PetroCaribe Fund, having turned the once bankrupt musician into a multi-millionaire, he supposedly is reappearing for elections in 2025!

-Why is the media glorifying acts of cannibalism that are staged, as if Haitians are truly cannibals?

-Toto Constant was a politician that supposedly hated the US. He was always badmouthing the United States. He turned out to be an American spy. Who would have thought of that? That created a real distrust in our society. For, while Toto Constant appeared to be vehemently anti-American, he was an agent in their pay. That Toto Constant was receiving money from Uncle Sam agents is unimaginable.

-There were a few attempts at destroying our folklore also. A good example is what happened when the United States occupied Haiti from 1915 to 1934. They introduced American Jazz in order to sell their products, destroying the local music industry. Voodoo was also declared illegal. It was called psychological warfare.

-Currently, Haiti has no President, no Legislature, having been deprived of Upper and Lower House. The Justice system is non-existent, despite the two-year stint of MINUJUSTH, or MINIJUPE, as Haitians call the United Nations Mission for the Support of Justice in Haiti, which replaced MINUSTHA in 2017. And the UN presence is still in Haiti, whatnot with the United Nations Integrated Office in Haiti, BINUH by its French acronym taking the baton from MINUJUSTH in 2019. Since then there has been some progress, with the Gang Federation, inaugurated in June 2020, having been facilitated by the slain President Moïse, who was applauded by the head of BINUH, Helen Ruth Meagher La Lime, then the representative of UN Secretary General António Guterres in Haiti.

With expansion of gangsterism, forget the existence of lawyers and medical doctors. There's always fuel scarcity affecting transportation in the country. The highways to the southern region of Haiti, as well as to the northern part, are blocked by gangs, hampering traffic between the capital and vast regions of the country. Moreover, streets in the capital itself are often blocked. The population is numbed and can no longer react.

-Even mother nature has no mercy on Haiti. The country has seen a litany of hurricanes. But the earthquake of 2010 was the coup de grace. That cannot be blamed on Haitians. Can bad luck be so extensive?

-No one in Haiti voiced an opinion or did something about Haiti's rice industry destroyed by President Bill Clinton, who, when he was UN envoy in Haiti after the 2010 earthquake, asked for forgiveness from the Haitian people. The Clintons must have loved Haiti. They had their honeymoon there. Yet, they participated in the destruction of Haiti! Why?

Haitians are so scared to talk or defend themselves nowadays, even those living in the diaspora, in the United States. But anywhere there is a Haitian there's disrespect of human rights. If you go to some local supermarket in a Haitian neighborhood in the USA, you will be asked to leave your bag outside, or give it to the store for storage until you get out. How is that for respect? No one other than President Clinton himself has mentioned this terrible damage to Haiti. I doubt that the Haitian American Lawyers Association has dealt with this.

-President Clinton was not the only guilty party in the devastation of the Haitian rice plantations, for the benefit of Arkansas rice farmers. He had some help. One of the conditions for President Aristide to return to power was to decrease the tariff on rice import from 35% to 10%. By agreeing, President Aristide was part of the devastation. I believe that President René Préval gave the "coup de grace" by decreasing the tariff to 3%, while the CARICOM organization of which Haiti is a member, has a tariff still at 30% on international products entering their Caribbean market. The Haitian peasants could no longer compete with imported rice price, the destruction of their rice fields was concretized. President Bill Clinton openly and officially apologized for destroying the Haitian rice production.

-There is now a report that the rice imported from Arkansas, Clinton's old state, has arsenic. So far, no Haitian or Haitian organization has tried to collect something from President Clinton or sue his organization for wrongdoing. That money would help in replanting the rice fields in Haiti. Considering that President Clinton has a lot of Haitian friends, how come none of them has asked him if he could do something in helping to restore the rice plantations in Haiti, for he himself admits his responsibility for their destruction.

-This one is very touchy. These two ladies Dr. Claudine Gay of Harvard University and University of Pennsylvania President Liz Magill had a very short answer sculpted specifically for the Congressional hearing regarding the conflict Israel-Hamas, obviously were advised by the lawyers of their universities. They used it and they lost their jobs. In reality it was not just a job. And we turned to Claudine Gay, the first Black woman named president of Harvard University, who has been a role model for the Haitian community. She did not take the heat on her own. All the Haitians felt it silently. Questions have been raised as to whether the lawyers of those universities are Jewish. Should the women have ignored the advice of their lawyers? How did little Haiti get mingled with big Israel? Haitians sincerely have missed their short-lived pinnacle with Claudine Gay's resignation. This is hard to understand, isn't it? Dr. Gay's nomination to the presidency of Harvard was vital to the health and pride of the Haitian people. Well, another big setback! No doubt, there are more to come.

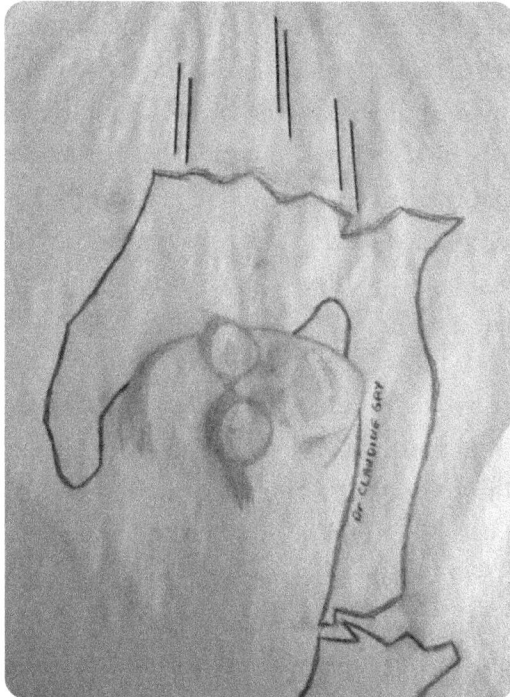

DRAWING by ARTIST KNOWN AS "S"
HAITI KEEPS FALLING, THERE SHOULD
BE A BOTTOM SOMEWHERE.

-All the main arteries of the country are blocked by the terrorists. Therefore, there is no need to continue planting or care for the land, if there is no harvesting or renumeration. Haiti's mango industry has greatly suffered. Due to gang activities, the companies preparing the fruits for export are barred from carrying out their duty, and Haitian mangoes, the best on the US market, no longer is found in fruit stores in America, reminiscent of what happened for two or three years, following the embargo imposed on Haiti, at the request of President Aristide when he was in golden exile in Washington in 1992-1994.

There is also a psychological warfare. There is an instinct of insecurity within self. The promotion of one-sided intelligence, yours is no good, only ours is good. The rejection of what looks like you. The constant bombarding of what you tend to assimilate with, so that you do not value it. The promotion of a God that doesn't look like you, to find out later from Russia that the saints were initially black and were painted white later. We also found out that the noses of the sphinx in the Egyptian pyramids have been destroyed intentionally, because they had large black noses. That implied that they were built by Blacks and that they had an advanced civilization in the early years of the world. What else have people done about which we know nothing, Haiti was destabilized and then paralyzed.

-There are so many inadvertent malefic decisions taken by the powerful in the world against Haiti that there's no wondering about whether it was intentional. Why couldn't the Haitian army import arms? Was Haiti going to fight with the Dominican Republic, Jamaica, Puerto Rico, Cuba, or the United States of America? Please tell me the rational of this act. There is the humiliation of putting the Haitian soldiers on the ground and handcuffing them when the army was being demobilized. The consensus was that Haiti did not need an army. There's one next door. By doing that, we've already shown that a vacuum was created which gave way to the bandit explosion.

Well, when all this chaos started, what did the powerful leaders of the international community do, so close by as they are? Now, those same leaders have proposed to send 1,000 policemen from Kenya to fix the problem, though they know that's not enough to make a dent in the insecurity. We had 8,000 to 10,000 blue helmeted soldiers of MINUSTAH in a relatively calm Haiti, and they did not help. How much do you think 10% of that number can accomplish? How can you maintain peace if you are just observing? In the case of the Kenyans, they can't shoot if they are not shot at. I explained this situation in the **GGTLM,** and stated that we would need at least 50,000 to 80,000 Haitian soldiers to stabilize the country. There should be a budget allocated to pay them, just as $400 million have been allocated for the Kenyans. One must stil ask: Will that help in doing something positive? El Salvador is much smaller than Haiti, yet more than $500 million were spent there to bring about security there. What is $400 million going to do in the Haiti case? An airplane ramp in Miami International Airport cost $7 billion. Cut my wings and prevent me from flying. Break my knees and prevent me from walking again. This is far from being coincidental.

-The more the African countries fight France, the faster Haiti will go down the hill, the more Haiti will suffer, because the former enslavers must continue to prove that real independence is not worth it. For, after two centuries of so-called independence, Haiti is the bad example not to follow. Thus, Haiti is being used to stop the full independence movement currently under way in West African countries. Oppressed countries must be reminded again and again about how horribly they will suffer, if they continue dreaming about freedom.

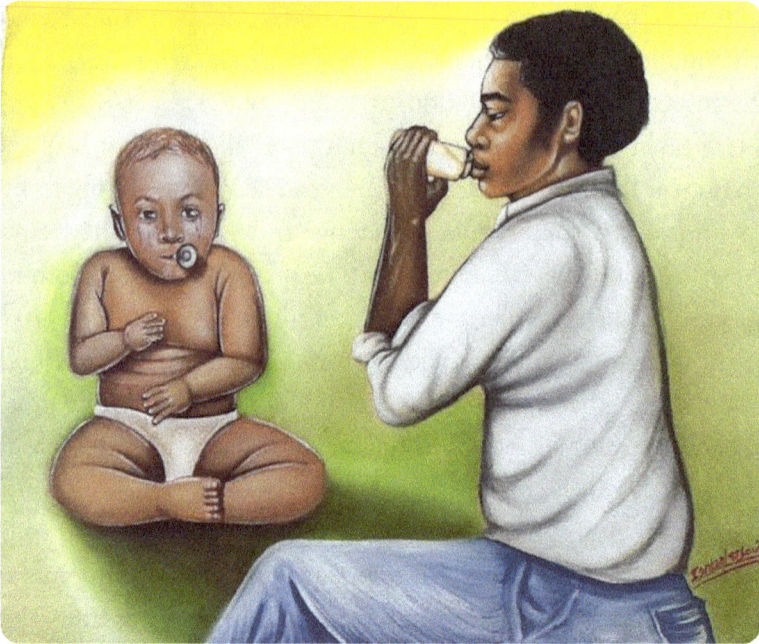

PAINTING by SILENT ARTIST
LETTING THE RAT WATCH THE CHEESE.

-Several heads of states have been killed or overthrown because they have tried to liberate their countries from the grip of colonialism and neocolonialism: Toussaint Louverture (France in 1803), Jean Jacques Dessalines (Haiti, in 1806), Um Nyobe (Cameroon, in1958), Barthelemy Boganda (Central African Republic, in 1959), Felix Moumie (Cameroon, in 1960), Sylvanus Olympio (Togo, in 1963), Eduardo Chivambo Mondlane (Mozambique, in 1969), Amilcar Cabral (Guinea-Bissau, in 1973), Marien Ngouabi (Republic of Congo, in 1977), Machel (Mozambique, in 1986), Thomas Sankara (Burkina Faso, in, 1987), Samuel Doe (Liberia, in 1990), Désiré Kabila (Congo, in 2001), Muammar Al-Gaddafi (Libya, in 2011).

In the history of Haiti, we already mentioned that the presidents who completed their mandates were in power during some kind of American occupation. The exception is Nissage Saget. The presidents, who were too promising in favor of their nation, were either assassinated or toppled. Papa Doc died of natural causes, but his son found himself on the way out the door, as Haiti registered, for the first time, a GDP of 5%. Precisely at a time that the country was making economic progress to get out of the hole. The GDP is now -2%. Whoever is/are the architects of this disaster must be happy.

By SILENT ARTIST
HAITIAN PRESIDENTS and
EMPEROR ASSASSINATED IN POWER

Haiti was the only place in the world where anyone of any color could come live without being frightened of retaliation. That is why Haiti is being extinguished right before our eyes.

I am not in the business of influencing people. This is public information. Make up your own mind.

Talking about the bandits, I may be doing something stupid, but it is undeniable that something is not adding up. I am just trying to understand the behavior of the bandits or terrorists. I will put it to them: If you are destroying everything on your path, whatever amount of money you've collected will not be of any use, because nothing would be left. Having destroyed everything, will you now eat the money? For, you will not find anything to buy. If you destroy the hospitals and the pharmacies, what will happen to you when you are hurt or fall sick? Then, where will you hide? Don't you think that it will catch up with you? Do you really believe that nobody will remember you and what you did? Don't you know that the people helping you in these horrible crimes will be the same ones to turn around and sell you out? It happened to Jesus, why wouldn't your buddies sell you out? Did it ever cross your mind that the friends laughing with you while you terrorize the population are inhaling your DNA from your cigarette buts, from your glasses, from your hair, and giving them to some authorities that will remain nameless? Let us see who will have the last laugh?

Looking at Haiti's infrastructure, you cannot believe it is in the Americas. I should not mention infrastructure. It is just a land devoid of almost everything useful. It's being completely destroyed. Perhaps it is better that way, because then it can be a land built from scratch.

WHAT REMAINS OF THE
CATHEDRAL IN PORT-AU-PRINCE

I am out of Haiti. So are my friends. They all have immigrated somewhere. The teachers/educators are out, gone to the USA, via the Biden immigration parole program. It's no different for the doctors and nurses, the lawyers, the farmers, the historians, the engineers, the law enforcement officials, the transportation workers; and the architects and builders have gone to the Dominican Republic. Who is left in the country? When you force everyone out, what will you do? You don't have the kind of knowledge to run the place. You don't understand this sophisticated new world. You cannot be isolated and think you can live in this world. You have to deal with the outside world. How will you go about making the deals that are a must?

Haiti is now a ghost country. Most French citizens don't know that Haitians fought and beat up their ancestors. They don't know that Haiti resulted from the first successful Black revolution. The Dominicans, next door, don't know that the island of Haiti, now called Hispaniola, belongs to both of us. In fact, most Dominicans don't know that Haitians liberated the Dominican Republic from the rule of the Spaniards. They don't know that the Dominican Republic was occupied by Haiti. If such important information is not in the books, then Haiti is a ghost country. Haiti never existed. If Haiti never existed, then there can't be any Haiti today. Such irreversible damages! The library of the Haitian government was ransacked and burned by gangs. That means all the papers that presidents and prime ministers have signed are no longer available to future generations, confirming that Haiti doesn't have a history. Indeed, Haiti doesn't exist anymore!

The emotion is still raw. Haiti is a country in ruins, only 800 miles from the shores of Florica, the most southeastern state of the United States of America. Some wonder about whether what is happening to Haiti is not an attempt to deliver Haiti to the Dominican Republic on a silver platter. What's the real plan? Is another population going to replace the Haitians just like the Jews moved to Israel? Or will Haitians be extinct just like the original inhabitants were exterminated after Christopher

Columbus supposedly discovered the island on December 5, called it "La Isla Española and laid claim on it for the queen of Spain?

You are not in an eastern European country during the so-called Cold War period. Still, you are scared of talking, because you don't want to be taken for a "rat," an offense punishable by death. Even death by burning! What a horrible life for poverty-stricken Haitians!

Someone rushed in to say they are burning the houses in the area. You hear the bullets flying. There is no time to grab anything. You don't close the door. You know better than that, if the door is closed it becomes a magnet. The bandits will think that there is something important in there. You want to save your life. For some time now, material belongings haven't had any meaning for you. No matter how short of breath you are, you pick up your baby and start running. You have forgotten that she is no longer a baby. She is 6 years old and weigh more than the baby you knew. But she didn't feel that heavy when you picked her up. It is the adrenaline. You realize all this when you got in the back of a truck that gave you a ride, quickly taking you away from the chaos. You were lucky, people do not stop to give a ride anymore. Now, you need a doctor, because you cannot breathe and have some chest pain. It doesn't matter because you're only thinking about finding a safe place to take your baby. A doctor visit is not an option anyway. Almost all of them have departed from the country. Even if you find someone with an ounce of medical knowledge, the pharmacies are empty, ransacked by the bandits. You would have been better off with a bullet in the chest. But the look on your baby's face made that idea ridiculous. At this point you know that God is good, despite the torture, you need to stay alive no matter what.

Haiti has reached a milestone, with 200 years of uninterrupted attack on its economy and on every fiber of Haitianhood. The current orchestrated insecurity has been like pouring gas continuously on the fire devouring Haiti. The country can't have a break. *"Nou pa ka pran youn souf,"* Haitians say in Creole. *(We can't take a breath of fresh air.)*

Another mea culpa. This one is coming from me. I was part of the ones saying that these people cannot read or write. Talking of the poor people of my country, I used to say that they don't know French. I used to laugh at the way they pronounce certain words. I used to call them sour mouth *(bouch si* in Creole). I didn't know that I was destroying my country by saying so. Instead of teaching them, I was putting them down. Now I know that the way I treated them was horrible, but I cannot go back and change things. Now they are the powerful. They found someone to give them authority. Now they have machine guns. Now they salute each other by saying: "Respect!" The respect that I did not give them. I had to leave the country in their hands, unable as they were. I knew they would have had much difficulty handling the situation. I really don't know what to expect. Did I expect them to do a better job than I? How could they, if they did not receive the education that they deserve? Yet, that doesn't give them the right to commit crimes as they are doing, almost nonstop. To tell the truth, I never thought that I was part of the problem until recently.

Many of us, Haitians, and a great number of Blacks around the world are suffering from a complex of inferiority. Haitians, specifically, suffer from Stockholm syndrome. They blame themselves for what has been done to them. If Blacks, all over the world, act a certain way, if Blacks, all over the world, act in a similar fashion, it means that something independent of them makes them act the way they do. It could be something genetic, but some Whites in the U.S. South have similar tendencies, a little less pronounced. Is it also genetic? Certainly, it's external.

Regarding the extent of insecurity in Haiti, the biggest problem is the inability of the people in charge to see or recognize the urgency of the matter. Previously said, I work in an emergency room of a hospital, and I can tell you that if a nurse or a doctor doesn't see a problem when it first emerges, it might be tackled too late. That is exactly what is happening in Haiti. It's taking too long for them to decide. It is taking too long for them to administer the remedy, while people are dying. They don't take into account that the medication itself takes a while to go into action. By the time they're done, they will leave the place in limbo, just as was done a few years back, following the exit of the MINUSTAH, (United Nations *Stabilization Mission in Haiti*. In not too distant a future, we will go back again to the same problems, because there's a new generation currently learning how to commit crimes by observing the bandits, while the leadership has not learned anything from mistakes committed in the past.

Haitians used to be so proud. They were proud of defeating Napoleon powerful army. When Belgium left Congo, the Haitians came to the rescue. They were proud to go educate the population. They were proud to be the first nation to be independent. They were proud to lead the way to the world freedom. They were proud to help multiple other countries to be independent. They were proud of their beaches. They were proud of their country's landscape. They were proud of their beautiful mountains. They were proud of their cuisine. They were proud of their beautiful woman. All this is fading away. Haiti is an impertinence that must be terminated.

These are events that have brought Haiti to its knees, The way Haiti has been destroyed by its own children allied to foreigners is a sacrilege!

CHAPTER 3

A LESSON FROM EL SALVADOR

El Salvador and the application of the greater good

After the undeniable success of the **GGTLM** book (the acronym for *"Gérard Germain, The Luckiest Man Who Grew Up in An Engineered and Manufactured Poverty,"* followed by *"Eiffel Tower, Pride of Haiti,"*

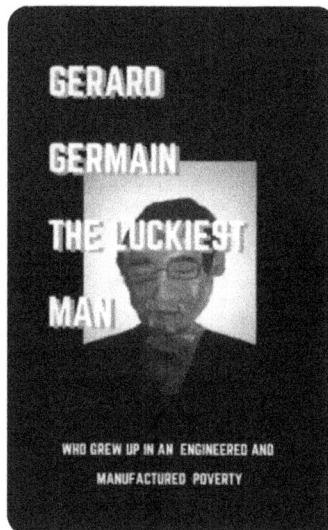

I have embarked in the search of truth regarding the newest form of rapid destruction of Haiti. The gang fever has been ravaging the country like many other unfortunate countries, but one country managed to control the violent unrest. El Salvador is the place to check out.

El Salvador is a Central American country, with a surface area of 21,041 square kilometers (km2) and a population of 6 million, which can be compared objectively to Haiti's surface of 27,750 square kilometers (km2) with a population of about 11 million.

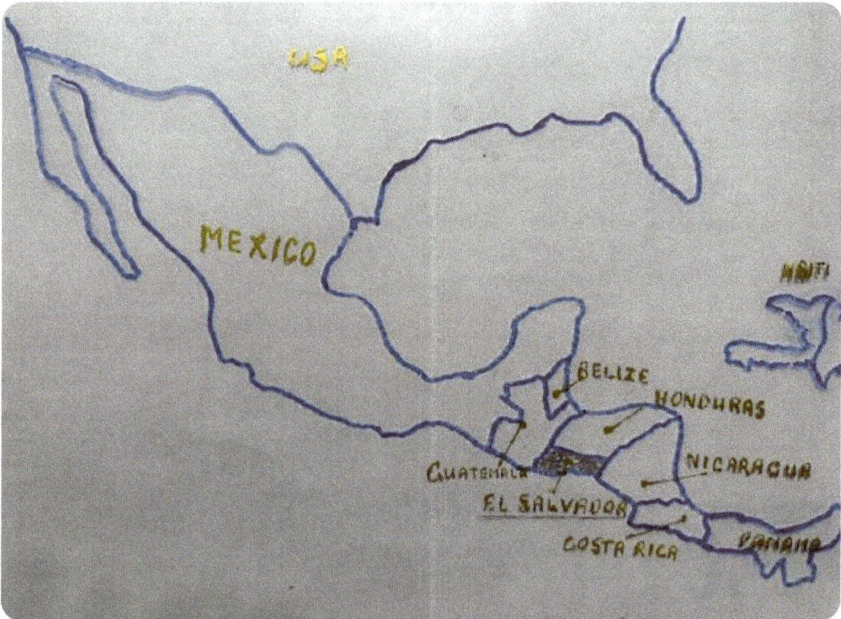

MAP OF CENTRAL AMERICA SHOWING
THE LOCATION OF EL SALVADOR.

It has been rumored that El Salvador has offered to help Haiti tackle the problem of insecurity. Considering that El Salvador has been very successful at eliminating the gang problem that brought the country to its knees, I decided to travel to El Salvador to get a briefing on how the leadership there had managed things.

I made the trip, especially, because I had some difficulty believing entirely social media reporting about the country. Even the international organizations and the traditional news media, sometimes, distorted what was going there and could not be fully trusted. I was determined to see with my own eyes the harm caused by terrorism. Also, I wanted to make a parallel between Haiti's current insecurity and that of Salvador and how the Salvadorian authorities manage to resolve the problem.

In 2019, El Salvador was reportedly the most dangerous country in the world. By 2024, El Salvador has managed to become the safest country of the Americas, as per Salvadorian President Nayib Bukele. Nonetheless, *worldreview.com,* quoting the Global Peace Index, is still reporting that Canada is the safest country in the Americas. Imagine that same index showing that Haiti is safer than the United States of America! No comments. I wanted to experience that freedom of ambulation in the street in San Salvador, the capital, after the tornado of insecurity. Then, I could confirm or refute the claims made in social and traditional media.

On my arrival in El Salvador, I spoke to the Vice President of the country, Dr. Felix Ulloa, a respectful, composed, and intelligent man. **Vice President Ulloa knows Haiti very well. Part of of his heart is there. He lived in Haiti for eight (8) years during the peace mission of the MINUSTAH, when he co-authored a book with Mirlande Manigat entitled: "Haiti: 200 years of Elections and Constitutions."** He is a driven person and must have strong opinions about the crimes that he is combating, because his father was assassinated, I was told. He is well versed in world issues. He's fluent in Spanish, French and English. He was educated in El Salvador (Banking and Finance), Spain (Law degree), France (Public Policy and Administration) and the United States of America (Public Affairs). This is the type of help that Haiti needed and still needs, and that was offered.

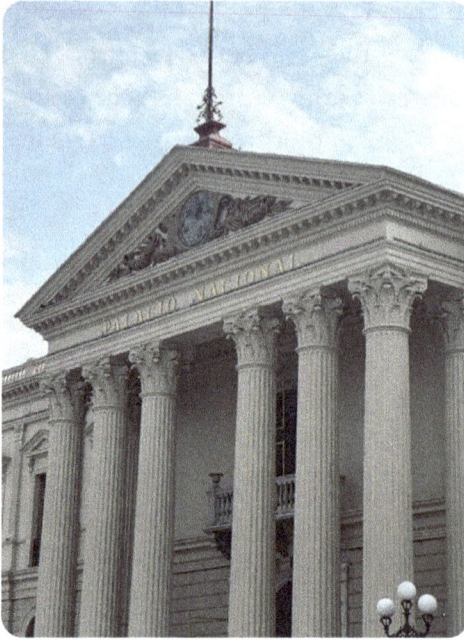

SALVADORIAN NATIONAL PALACE

He arranged for a meeting with me at his office/residence, but had to make changes at the last minute, due to previous engagements on that day which was Mother's Day, also a Salvadorian holiday. My interview, therefore, was with his Chief of Staff. I met with *"El Director General de Gabinete de la Vicepresidencia, Señor Mario Otero."*

Meeting with the Chief of Staff of the Vice President of El Salvador

Like his boss, he is well versed in Haiti's situation. We discussed Haiti and spoke about coordinating efforts to stabilize security in Haiti, as was achieved in his country. We took pictures between two chairs with the "Coat of Arms" of El Salvador on the cushion of the chairs and carved also on the wooden head rest with the Salvadorian Flag in the background at a corner of the room.

He told me that El Salvador has been asked by many countries how they were able to neutralize the gangsters. He explained that every country is not the same and what works for one might not work as well for another. He also insinuated that the people in charge must be willing to sacrifice something to reach their desired goal. There is so much criticism from all angles. Nothing of what I mention here is a direct quote.

I asked him if it is true that the Salvadorian government had offered to help with the gang problem in Haiti.

WITH THE CHIEF OF STAFF MARIO OTERO
OF THE VICE PRESIDENT OF EL SALVADOR FELIX ULLOA.

He told me that though the Salvadorian authorities offered to help, they cannot act on their own. They must receive a mandate from the United Nations, which would require a request from the Haitian government. The offer was apparently unofficial, and the Haitian government had to also ask. I know there was an offer. I read about it in an article in the Miami Herald by Odelyn Joseph which was a based on one by

Jacqueline Charles, on January 30, 2023, entitled; *"Haiti needs help fighting gangs, El Salvador has had success and is offering help,"* The offer was to "send an assessment mission to the Caribbean nation to prepare a comprehensive proposal on how to solve the security and gang crisis in Haiti," As per Mr. Joseph, the offer was made at a Community of Latin American and Caribbean States Summit in Buenos Aires by Doctor Felix Ulloa Garay, the Salvadorian Vice- President. He had met Doctor Ariel Henry, then Prime Minister of Haiti. Mind you, Vice-President Ulloa already knew the territory, as previously stated. Haiti just had to ask. But until he was forced to resign by actions of the gangs, Ariel Henry, a neurosurgeon, could not figure this out and never asked. Maybe what Haiti needs is just a second opinion. The first doctor had failed.

Back to Chief of Staff Mario Otero. He mentioned a second but important issue. He said that the presidency in El Salvador was currently in a transitional period. In El Salvador, for an incumbent to run for reelection, power must be transferred to a third party for six months. Then, if reelected, power is transferred back to that incumbent government on inauguration day, which is June 1st. That is the law of the land. Though strange, it does make sense. This should normally prevent any incumbent from fixing the results of the election. Nothing could have been done anyway between January and June 2024.

I mentioned that the 3rd obstacle could be that no one wants the situation to change, allowing improvement of the condition for the Haitian people. He did not deny it, but did not officially comment about that, the subject being so fluid and multidimensional.

My six senses have been active:

Coming out of the office of the Vice-President of El Salvador, after my conversation with his Chief of Staff, I asked myself some questions. My sixth sense has been very active. Here are some of them:

To fix the insecurity problem, wouldn't we need someone that has experience in that matter? Who would be more qualified to resolve a complex situation like the one we face in Haiti, than someone who has been in Haiti, or someone who is learning the process of helping? Who would be the best adviser, if not someone who has successfully neutralized the bandits who are similar to our gangs? Should we rely on personalities that have not resolved any problem of insecurity in their own country or on those that have 85% approval of their population for the task well done? The choice is clear. El Salvador can help us.

BOUKELE = **BOUKLE BANDI YO** (Boukele buckled them up)

Why didn't we ask El Salvador (The Savior) for help? When they offered to help, why didn't we accept the offer? Voices in my head keep asking me: Who has interest in the demise of Haiti? Who are the Suspects? What could Haiti be good for, that we know nothing about? Could some entity be planning on changing the population of the country? Could some entity be holding the country captive for some strategic advantage? Could there be a recolonization plan? Could there be a plan of Black extermination? Could some multi-billionaire be planning on buying Haiti for pennies on the dollar? Nvidia has a market cap of 2+ trillion dollars and counting. That is not in the realm of the impossible. It seems that the plan is to keep Haiti the way it is right now.

Well! I wore my Sherlock Holmes skeptical hat and took a special trip all the way to San Salvador to investigate and discuss with the experts and digest what I have learned.

I still wanted a second layer of convincing that the El Salvador example could help Haiti. Curious as I am, I still wanted to see more and hear more.

I took to the streets of San Salvador, the capital. The name of the city is derived from the name of the patron saint of the city: *"San Salvador del*

Mvndo". This is not a misprint. The name of the saint is written with a "v" instead of a "u" in *mundo* which means world. The whole name would be in English: *Saint Savior of the world.*

SAN SALVADOR DEL MVNDO

My first stop was the newly constructed 7-story library called: *"Biblioteca Binaes."* I wanted to have a conversation with a Salvadorian historian. They could not refer me to one. However, I was able to freely talk to some people in the library.

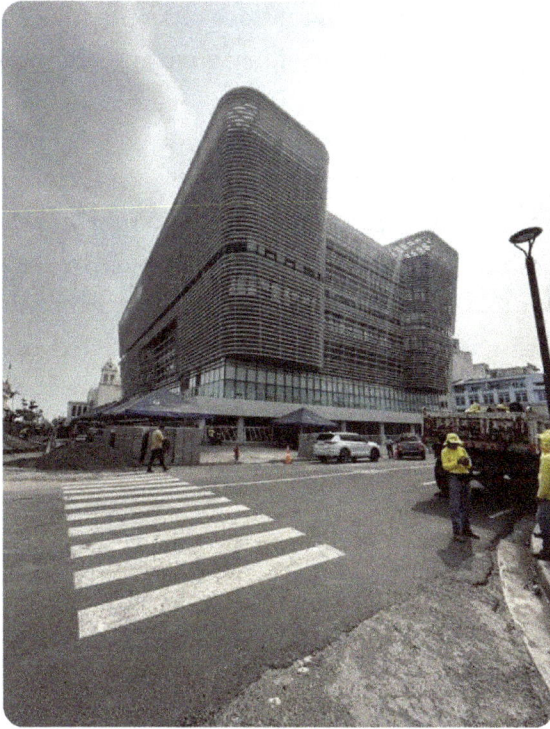

BIBLIOTECA BINAES
A 7 FLOOR LIBRARY

That day I also realized that there was a police sub-station in the street under a tent, in front of a bank with two ambulatory police officers and two police officers on motorcycles. Security and safety are tangible, I told myself. You can see it. You can smell it. You can almost touch it.

I started talking to everyday people.

I was told by Alexander, my first encounter, that the government knew where these people lived. He meant the bandits. The government scanned the country's neighborhood one after the other. They went to their homes between 2 and 5 am. All the bandits and accomplices were arrested without firing a bullet, because the police knew who they were and where they lived. The bandits also could not get rid of their tattoos that fast. As it is, it's not illegal to have tattoos in El Salvador.

I met three guys with significant tattoos on their skins. Their tattoos, however, were not of gang style. They were ambulating freely in the capital of the country.

Salvadorians to whom I spoke are unanimous in their appreciation of what was done with the gang issue. Such comments were expressed by people who had relatives in the mega jails built by the government. One taxi driver told me that if someone is seen in company of a *pandilla* (gang member in Spanish), that person is also arrested and questioned. The sentence applied in that case is less than that reserved for *pandillas*. Some *pandillas* have been jailed for 20 years, others for life, with no parental visit, if you please. No phone calls, no letters or mail for the prisoners, I was told. They have no access to the internet. Families have the option of buying them a package that includes underwear, socks, sandals, etc.

The Human Rights activists are in an uproar, due to what they consider mistreatment of *pandillas,* but the population is adamant, blurting out their feelings. Some say imagine how they feel when they no longer can call or send a letter to family members that have been killed by the bandits. Why, then, should the bandits have the rights to such privilege? If the criminals have all those rights, what are the rights of the population? Which one is the greater good?

My taxi driver told me that he lost family members that have been killed by the gangs. He doesn't understand why the political opposition is talking about the rights of the bandits, while he did not have any right when the bandits were exercising their power over the population. As it was, Organized Crime was out of control in El Salvador. During the peak of Mafia time, since it was a rather small portion of the population involved in that, it was bearable. Then, every neighborhood became involved in criminal activity, which was no longer a hobby, but a job. When too many people are involved in doing it, the authorities must do something about it.

Edwin talked about a house he had built, to the cost of $35,000. The gangs took it away from him and sold it. Now he cannot get his house back, because the people living in it have fake papers that cannot be contested.

Miguel lost his life savings in the process. The money was invested in his wife cosmetology business. Young kids that grew up in his neighborhood that he knew and that knew him well, came to the business, they ransack the place, took what they wanted and left. He rebuilt the business, and the same thing kept happening until there was no more money.

Louis said that if you had a daughter during that era, they would force her to be part of the gang or force you to give the daughter away to them as girlfriend of one of the gang members. You had the choice of either giving away your daughter, and she could, at times, visit the family, or they would steal her, and you wouldn't see her again, ever. In such a circumstance, you would run out of luck anyway, because by giving her away, your daughter would end up in in jail as an accomplice. Remember, there are no family visitors allowed in for jailed gang members.

I found out that no one knew that the government was building a mega jail to house the gangs. When Mr. Bukele was running for president, he didn't promise anything about jailing the gangs. But he had gained experience by having been mayor of two different cities prior to becoming president. Now as president, he was about to show his mettle. Though he attended Law School, he didn't graduate. Certainly, he deserves an honorary diploma for all his accomplishments. Which goes to show that one doesn't necessarily need a lot of diplomas to undertake major tasks. No need for all sorts of qualifications. What you need is the will to change things and be surrounded by people in the know who are dedicated to the cause at hand.

Another Salvadorian I spoke to is Maria. She gave me a vivid story of a gang member that came to her house one night, knife drawn and asking for money. He had that large knife on her mother's throat. The mother found a way and the courage to catch the knife and direct it away from her. She was bleeding heavily in the hand with which she had grabbed the knife. The father took that opportunity to enter the battle. The two dogs in the house also showed their discontent of what was happening. After some pushing and shoving the bandit was on the ground as there were a total of four family members in the house, including my friend. He was tied down and the police was called. It took a while for the police to arrive, but they finally came. The terrorist swore to come back for revenge. Revenge for what, I would ask. They did not entice him. They did not entrap him. He just went to the wrong house. He was messing with the wrong people.

They taught that was the end of the story. But a few days later, someone rang the bell late at night. From the window, the father looked out. He was shaking when he saw that the house was surrounded by bandits. The head of that group told him that he came to kill him and burn the house because of the incident that happened the other day. During the conversation, a kid, member of the gang came to my friend's dad and asked him if he remembered him. How could he forget? This kid used to come to the house daily to eat. He shook his head trying to say yes but the words would not come out. The kid told him that he was safe. He was only asked to remove the complaint so that the prisoner could be released. He had no choice but to comply. My friend was crying, when telling me the story of that event which occurred five years earlier.

Jaime feels that without the government requesting it, the people are following the principle of *"See something, Say something"* as the American motto goes. When they feel that things are suspicious, they take a picture of it, put it on the internet and notify the authorities.

Jose, another man I met in El Salvador told me that his goal, when growing up, was to live up to 30 years of age. He never taught or dreamed of being a lawyer, a doctor, or a schoolteacher. His ultimate dream was just to live to be 30. It was so dangerous, that he did not see pass 30 years in his future. So many bad things had happened in his younger years. His older brother who was the patriarch of the family, because his father died when he was 4 years old, one day left the house to work and never came back. He vanished completely. At that time, this was a current occurrence and it was assumed that he became a victim of the *pandillas*. Since his brother disappeared, his mother was never the same. She died two years after that event. Therefore, my friend was sure that he would die before he reached his 30th anniversary. However, he made it to 32 years and has two daughters.

As for Miguel, who lost a small fortune in his wife's cosmetology business, this whole gang problem started with the 12-year war between the government of El Salvador and the FMLN *(Farabundo Marti National Liberation Front)*. Unofficially, the peasants were upset because of low pay by the rich and the oligarchs. They revolted. Some were killed by the government after the murder of Archbishop Oscar Romero Galdamez, during a mass. A domino effect brought a war of 12 continuous years with even the involvement of Cuba and the Soviet Union, now known as Russia. Many fathers lost their lives during that war. Thus, many kids grew up without their dad, devoid of a role model. Some ended going to the United States for refuge. While there, for territorial protection, they formed gangs like MS13 *(Mara Salvadoran, Mara Salvatrucha)*. (Mara meaning friend, gang). Incidentally Mara in Hebrew means bitter. The number 13 was used for the name of their original street, considered their territory. In the 1980s, MS13 originated at 13th Street, in Los Angeles, California. There are also other gangs, such as *Barrios 18*. Most of the gangs had a similar existential model an modus operandi.

Since MS13 members were easily identifiable by their tattoos, they were deported to El Salvador after the end of the Salvadorian civil war, in 1992. On arrival in their country of origin, they continued their illicit activities and almost took over the control of some parts of El Salvador.

I visited the Monument of Truth *(Monumento de la Verdad)*, erected for the 75,000 people who died during the civil war which lasted from 1980 to1992. It was a very touching experience.

Delinquency brought tourism in El Salvador down to null. Understandbly so, because tourists were often robbed and assaulted. No one dared make a cell phone call while out in the street. That phone would be stolen, and you would be assaulted. Now tourism has increased by 30%. There is *"audiovisual vigilante,"* where regular people post videos on social media of acts of malfeasance that they've witnessed. The fear of reprisal has since abated. Do you think they would be able to have a "Miss Universe Pageant" in the most dangerous country of the world? El Salvador just staged one. I couldn't believe that safety was established so rapidly. But I have witnessed it. I walked in rich as well as in poor sections of El Salvador. I did watch my back, but that's what I do in the United States of America also, not because I was fearful or uncomfortable. Right now, San Salvador, the capital of El Salvador is a vast construction site and is very safe.

Is there an El Salvador in Haiti's history?

A FRESH FRUIT STAND IN THE OPEN MARKET IN EL SALVADOR

THE LESS FORTUNATE AREAS OF SAN SALVADOR ARE AS
SAFE AS THE AFFUENT ONES, I NOTED DURING MY WALK.

CHAPTER 4

SALVADOR AND HAITI: COMPARE AND CONTRAST

I decided to make some comparison between El Salvador and Haiti:

(SALVADOR FLAG) Salvador has a government. Had an election. (HAITI FLAG) Haiti has no government. No elected officials since November 2016.

(SALVADOR FLAG) Salvadorian gangs originated in the United States. A great number of them were in jail in the US and were repatriated. (HAITIAN FLAG), A lot of the gang members were repatriated after committing crime in the United States.

(SALVADOR FLAG) Salvadorian bandits were using handguns, pistols, knives and other pain producing instruments. They were powerful and ubiquitous. They were like the gangs abusing populations all over the world. (HAITIAN FLAG) Haitians gangs got their hands on drones, AR15, AK47, matches to burn everything in their path, including human beings. They are heavily armed by an inconspicuous party(s). Haitian gangs' actions are chaotic, often one cannot tell or understand their action. Could they be doing things just because? Because of what?

It's not at all clear. Their collecting capability is impressive, but gauged by their outfits, apparently they still have no money.

(SALVADOR FLAG) Salvadorian gang members almost invariably had visible tattoos. Some have their gang ID letters or numbers. Sometimes the letter and number are visibly tattooed on their skin. Apparently, that was instrumental in identifying the gang members. I am almost sure that some youngsters have tattooed themselves for notoriety and protection, without belonging to any gang. Now they have become collateral damage. After the successful operation by the Salvadorian government, probably the tattoo parlors went bankrupt. The tattoos made the *pandillas* easily recognizable, facilitating their arrest when the government undertook action against them, landing them in jail. (HAITIAN FLAG) In Haiti the gang bosses are frequently on social media. They are, therefore, easily identifiable. Some of their followers, however, have their heads and faces covered. The question here is who is the real boss? Some gang members do have tattoos, but it is difficult to notice because of their dark skin color.

(SALVADOR FLAG) There are judges who, intentionally or accidentally, show leniency toward gang leaders. Some, not unlike certain politicians, were on the payroll of the gangs. Other judges were scared for their lives and the safety of their family and felt obliged to comply with the demands of the gangs. Some of those unscrupulous officials also have been arrested to make peace possible. (HATIAN FLAG) Many politicians have been implicated in crime, but the justice system is almost non-existent. It has been difficult to address these issues in an orderly fashion. Some politicians are just puppets on the string.

(SALVADORIAN FLAG) In El Salvador there were territorial fights. Also, there were crimes of opportunity. (HAITIAN FLAG) In Haiti, the crimes are even more baseless and crueler. People are beaten up and burned alive. The terrorists in Haiti would kick some victims out of their homes, not necessarily taking anything from the residences, just burn them down. This means that they did not need the house to begin with. What is also interesting and puzzling with the crisis in Haiti is that the victims are neighbors, old friends, cousins, parents of friends of the bandits. Haiti also has seen a lot of rape. A novel sight: Barricaded streets, so the gangs may collect toll or ransom. Totally illegal, such collection is done with the risk of death, which is common. If one dares to object, it's death on the spot. One can also witness his/her vehicle being burned down to the tires with a Molotov cocktail.

(SALVADORIAN FLAG) El Salvador was able to place cameras in suspicious areas of the highways or main roads to monitor the criminals. In the blink of an eye, the police would be dispatched to evaluate any potential situation. I found out that the cameras were instrumental at identifying some activities of the *pandillas*. El Salvador has electricity 24 hours a day, facilitating this task. It's a country with many volcanos that are used as thermal energy to produce electricity. (HAITIAN FLAG) Haiti has no electricity. Haiti has no money. There is no public video monitoring.

(SALVADORIAN FLAG) El Salvador government was able to determine with clarity the site of extortion. They waited for the gang members when they came to collect regular ransom money. They were able to find out where the exchange of money was taking place. (HAITIAN FLAG) The collections are made at different sites and any police activity is easily detected by the bandits. Remember that the bandits have more firing power than the police.

(SALVADORIAN FLAG) El Salvador has a strong army and police force now. That was not always the case. A Salvadorian at the hotel where I stayed told me that the president had to put pressure on Congress to get enough money to increase the capacity of the army, in weapons et all. (HAITIAN FLAG) Haiti is still under an American arm embargo, while the bandits have machine guns galore. Haiti also has no government. The government is in charge only on paper.

AR15, ONE OF THE PREFERED WEAPONS
OF THE HAITIAN GANGS.

(SALVADOR FLAG) El Salvador used to have its own currency, called the Colon. They are no longer using the Colon. They use the US dollar, just as is done in Puerto Rico and Panama. The money is in the bank, a Salvadorian official told me, they just have not used them. (HAITIAN FLAG) Using the American Dollar as currency was one of my propositions for Haiti in the **"Gerard Germain, The Luckiest Man** book. The Haitian *"Gourde"* has been devaluated constantly and consistently ever since it was unlinked from the US dollar.

(SALVADOR FLAG) Even with the strong police presence, some private institutions are still using private guards. Case in point is the hotel where I stayed that had a guard at the entrance on a 24-hour basis. (HAITIAN FLAG) This makes me believe that the private security business in Haiti can still survive, even with the return to a semi normalcy. The security business in Haiti is very powerful and would not appreciate any change that would put it out of business.

(SALVADORIAN FLAG) The government was able to confiscate the phones of the terrorists who were arrested and, decoding them, were able to find much about them, including who are their friends and sympathizers. That was helpful in making important connections that was key in the success of the government's security program. Just like in Haiti, many of the criminals, especially those used as lookout, operate under cover. These undercover criminals were also passive acquaintances who benefited from the ascent of the bandits and never dared to tell them that what they were doing was wrong. Some family members and friends knew that the terrorists were killing people and still aided them, due to financial remuneration, for the dirty money was shared directly or indirectly with them. With information obtained from the cellphones, the authorities investigated those who were called often by the bandits. They checked the messages sent and received. They learned the coded language of the gangs when sending messages. They monitored their schedules, kept tab on them on social media. (HAITI FLAG) The phone system in Haiti is impracticable and unreliable. Thus, the bandits use other archaic forms of communication. There is also the problem of financing. Haiti has no money to afford the complicated web of monitoring mentioned. The country has been paralyzed for years, making it difficult for anything to be accomplished.

The government of El Salvador also took some risks. El Salvador is one of the rare countries where crypto currency is accepted. The government created its own bitcoin wallet called *"Chivo"* and donated $30 of crypto to every one of the 6 million citizens. Investing and using crypto currency was a big risk. Whether you agree or not, crypto currency is very speculative and unstable. Bitcoin, the first crypto currency valued in October 2009, was worth $ 0.0009. Now, one bitcoin is worth around $60,000 to $70,000. At this point, ARK Investment Management speculates that one bitcoin will be worth one million dollars ($1,000,000.00) in 2030. This would defeat any laws known to us. That's why all the central banks and the Federal Reserve Bank don't like the idea of a currency that is not backed up by any means known to men. There are over 4,000 crypto currencies available, without any standard regulations. Moreover, up to now the inventor of bitcoin, Satoshi Nakamoto, is a questionable entity. His or their identity is not known. Therefore, accepting the volatile crypto currency was taking a chance, indeed a big one! I must agree that in taking that risk, the government was very lucky, because it's working.

To make sure that the information I gathered was accurate, I spoke to a few Salvadorians living in South Florida. Just in case the people that I met in El Salvador were afraid to badmouth the government, I spoke to some who patronize the *"Atlakat Restaurant"* in South Florida. The results were the same. People are genuinely happy about being alive, expressing it in sighs of relief. This is also seen as a catalyst for progress. People are so proud of the accomplishments of their new government and country. The feeling is overwhelmingly good.

CHAPTER 5

HOW DID THEY DO IT OFFICIALLY?

For El Salvador to come out of the situation in which it was, the leadership came up with a plan of "Territorial Control" which included:

1. Getting out of the list of countries of the world which were more violent in 2021.
2. Have the elements to make the war against the gangs possible.
3. Guarantee that the peace is possible in the long term.

It was budgeted to cost about $ 500 million in 2019. It was an elaborate anti-gang program, which included six (6) phases. There was a backup 7th phase, in case of failure of the prior 6. The first phase started in June 2019 and the last phase ended in September 2023, but still ongoing. This was the first successful program at decreasing the power of the gangs. Since early in 2000, every Salvadorian President has implemented social programs to combat crime and the gangs. They have not all been successful. For example, there have been hardened critics of the Territorial Control program, who state that the decrease in homicides was just following a trend. Others have stated that the president is acquiring power by militarizing the country.

The 6 phases of the Territorial Control are noted below and were implemented in 3 months.

1. PREPARATION: The presence of police and army personnel wherever gang financial transactions are performed. State of emergency in prisons, through complete lockdown, no use of cell phone, and no visitation.
2. OPPORTUNITY: Education, health care, building of schools and sport centers to give options to the young and stop young blood from feeding the gangs.
3. MODERNIZATION: Improved police patrols and more updated weapons for the army and police.
4. INCURSION: Entering the strongholds of the gangs, which was inaccessible before.
5. EXTRACTION: Extract the gang members hidden in the community and construction of a mega jail to relieve overcrowding.
6. INTEGRATION: formation of the National Department of Integration.

Phase 7 is still a secret.

At any favorable occasion, the president of El Salvador would add more members to the military and the police. Monthly homicide rate in the country was 2.4 per 100,000, in 2023, whereas in 2019, it was 50 per 100,000. The top year for homicides in El Salvador was 2015, when the monthly rate was 104 murders per 100,000 inhabitants. That amounted to 5,100 murders that year. Compared that to 0 (zero) murder monthly per 100,000 in Monaco and 43 per 100,000 in 2023 in Haiti. Mind you, crimes are under-reported in Haiti and sometimes people are left dead on the ground for more than 24 hours. The situation has worsened. No one knows what the rate could be now.

Cell phone robberies were once rampant in El Salvador. One could not make a cell phone call on the street. Reports of cell phone theft was a constant on the national news networks. Now, you can show off your cell phone, even carry and expensive one. Unafraid, girls go about using their beautified cell phones any time.

Vigilance has not dropped in El Salvador. Hotels and banks are still using arm guards. That makes me believe that the security business in Haiti will survive a successful reform, leading to a lengthy period of stability and peace.

A walk in the open mall

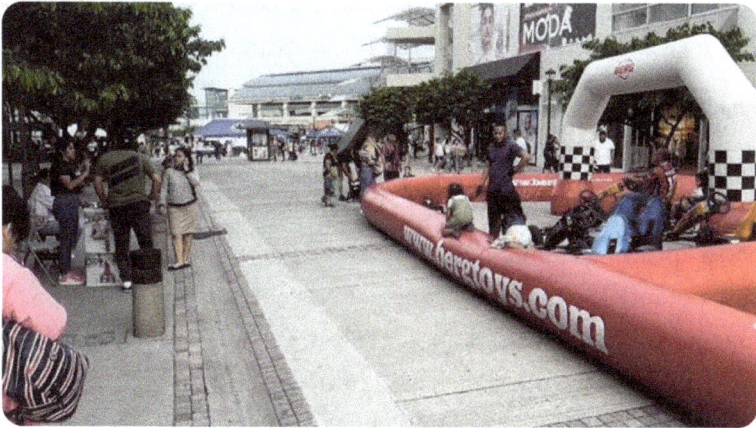

FAMILIES ENJOYING THE AFTERNOON AT
"LA GRAN VIA" TILL MIDNIGHT

It was a difficult assent to power for Nayib Bukele, who had failed getting acceptance as a candidate under the banner of several Salvadorian parties. Ultimately, he ended up organizing his own party called *"Nuevas Ideas"* (New Ideas) to run for president.

When I sat down with Mario Otero, the Chief of Staff of the El Salvador Vice-President at the latter's office-residence, as previously mentioned, he made it clear that they were following the laws of the land. They needed the power of the army to neutralize the *pandillas*. So they did just that. Security was their priority. One can tell that they succeeded because the police presence was clearly noted and still, as I, personally, have noted. We went over some of the tactics that were used by the administration of President Bukele. Without going into minuscule details, things began by first restraining the bandits and finally incarcerate them. The way I understand it, they were able to identify the gang members and accurately determine their strongholds. Tackling the insecurity at the outset was the principal goal of the actual president. Obviously, that has paid off. But it was no walk in the park. As noted earlier, there has been much criticism of President Bukele. Yet, other countries have been trying to find out how El Salvador accomplished what has been done. Some countries want to apply a similar formula, because, obviously it's working.

Mr. Otero emphasized that the same system may not be applicable in other countries. The will to bring about change must exist. In fact, it's more important than any of the obstacles to be encountered in the process. Speaking about Haiti, we were not able to come up with a specific potential solution. Of course, I was not there in the capacity of a Haitian government official. Nonetheless, we both agreed that nothing substantial can be undertaken in Haiti, without bringing insecurity under control by getting the Haitian people involved in the process. As it is, there's nothing to gain by speaking to a Haitian living in Haiti about human rights. Since life itself is banalized, there can't be any human rights. For sure, some people advocate human rights for all, while denying the rights to the population. They are the criminals, the bandits, the terrorists and gangs. The concept of human rights, as it's known and respected in the developed world, is not applicable in an underdeveloped country like Haiti. We need education first, before full blown human rights may be enforced.

Looking at El Salvador today, compared to what it was previously, it is the best place for real estate investment of which one can think. Due to many years of internal wars, it was a cheap deal, especially when the locals evacuated and moved to neighboring countries. It wasn't that difficult because they all speak the same Spanish language and have the same physiognomy. Now with the insecurity resolved, and the confidence of the population fully restored, the Salvadorian diaspora, with their significant buying power, is buying land and real estate. Prices have gone up considerably but are nowhere close to what they should have been or what the neighboring countries charge.

Coming to El Salvador, one automatically realizes that there is a way out of the disarray. One is struck by the rapidity in improvement of the situation. Hope is in the air, everyone is happy about the changes, which are obvious. Imagine that even people who have some relatives in jail and can't still see them, because prison visit isn't allowed, are happy that there's been an end to the cancer that was destroying the country. Double that, if you are Haitian. Just don't do anything stupid about which you'll regret later. Think before acting, because you have plenty time to reflect. Consider that if you are underage, you go to a special prison. When you become 18 you're transferred to a regular prison for 15 more years. As it is, the justice system is overwhelmed, due to the number of delinquents roaming in the streets. Moreover, there were a lot of bad people acting up. And a lot of good people learned how to be bad because it was profitable. There seems to be a big fight here now for the greater good. El Salvador was saved by *San Salvador Del Mundo*. So far, this guy talks about President Bukele as a gift from heaven. He seems genuine. We hope he doesn't change, the taxi driver Miguel told me.

Let us hope I can use these same words talking about Haiti in two years.

Let me recapitulate:

El Salvador – Haiti – Kenya

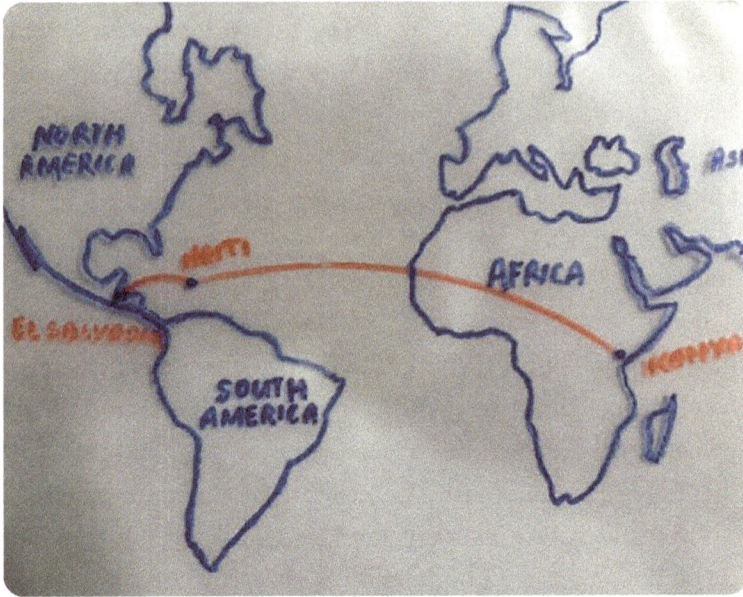

Distance between El Salvador and Haiti: 1,182 miles.
Distance between Kenya and Haiti: 7,485 miles.

With El Salvador (The Savior) you have the advantage of something that is already working as opposed to something you will be experimenting with Kenya. El Salvador is 6 times closer to Haiti than Kenya. The Vice-President of El Salvador knows Haiti, for having lived there for eight (8) years. The Haitian landmark is familiar to them. You decide which is potentially the best choice for Haiti, even if you have no say in the matter.

People have a short memory, after a few years of being complacent, people will forget what they have. The people of El Salvador will forget how bad life was once. I hope the people of El Salvador do not forget what they did not have and remember what they now have. Hopefully Haiti is no longer the Haiti of today then. I hope that Haiti does not remain a reminder for you Salvadorian of how bad things can be like when you are complacent and trust human beings blindly.

Remember, MS13, or whoever your enemies are, did not disappear. They are just regrouping. One mega-prison can be broken into, and all your enemies can be freed in a blink of an eye. Spread them so that they cannot be all out at one time. Be on the lookout for them, they are not far. They are within you.

CHAPTER 6

NO UNTANGLING THE FRENCH ETERNAL NOOSE

The country that invented freedom and liberty is now humiliated. Freedom vanished in Haiti. Could there be a connection to African countries waking up that must be convinced that freedom is not going to take them anywhere but in the current circumstances in which Haiti has found itself?

Haiti had to pay at gunpoint for the loss of slaves to the French former slave owners. That was an insult to Haiti and Blacks in general.

Isn't it humiliating for Haiti to have recently received a gift of 17 motorcycles from France to combat the insecurity caused by the gangs? The motos are not propelled by hydrogen or nuclear energy. They are 17 regular motorcycles. It's not a gift to a small business. Neither to an individual. It is a gift to a country with 11 million people. The staff at the embassy of France in Port-au-Prince could come up with a more valuable present just by pinching in from what they could pull out of their own pockets. But I will not blame France in this situation. I blame the department in Haiti that accepted the motos. Shame on you!

Why is CARICOM (Caribbean Community and Common Market) making decisions about and for Haiti? Isn't Port-au-Prince the biggest capital in the CARICOM alliance? Is it in CARICOM's interest for Haiti to get better? Asking a bunch of small countries to dictate how Haiti must be run is humiliating. Mind you, these countries are not really independent themselves. The King of England is the Head of State of most of them. CARICOM is supposed to be a common market that implies a financial organization. Why are they making political decisions? Since they are creating precedents, will they accept other countries in the region, like Haiti, to make decisions for them? Do they realize this is what they just did? They just invited Haiti to help them make political decisions in the future.

The plan for Haiti was dictated by CARICOM. There is a rumor that the candidate for the CPT (Conseil Présidentiel de Transition) that will run the country for at least two years had to sign the document and would follow what has been "proposed." In this case, what has been "ordered" would have been a more appropriate wording.

This little country that was able to leave a footprint in the history of the world cannot get lucky, not even once. We got a Prime Minister that can be classified as one of the smartest individuals in the world. For God's sake, the guy is a neurosurgeon! He was nominated by President Jovenel Moïse whom we found out was doing his best for the country. To be nominated, he must have had a great plan. Well, there was no execution of any plan during his almost three years in power. Who knows what he signed when he realized that he could not return to Haiti.

I understand, what's in your mind is gospel truth for you. One of my dearest and closest family members, born in Haiti, raised in Haiti and educated there, is French. She is French in the flesh, mentally and spiritually. Her clothing is French. Her culture is French. Her preferred cuisine is French. In her book, the French cannot do anything wrong. She calls herself *"les bleus,"* a French flattering connotation.

Isn't it insulting for the President of the United States, Joseph "Joe" Biden, to meet with the President of the Dominican Republic, then meet with the President of Kenya, regarding Haiti while never meeting any Haitian authority regarding Haiti itself? Please, tell, isn't that insulting? No money, no respect! That's how it works? In the USA, we keep thinking that the Democratic Party is the party of Blacks, but President Barack Obama himself did something similar. He was President of the United States of America for eight (8) years. He visited Jamaica, a good Caribbean friend of the United Staes, and Puerto Rico, a U.S territory in the Caribbean, He visited Cuba, supposedly in the enemy camp. The head of State then, Raul Castro, did not even bother to come out to greet him at the airport where he had just greeted the Pope. But Obama didn't set foot in Haiti, the country which really made it possible for him to be President of the United States. Air Force One never landed with him aboard, even for five minutes, on the tarmac at the Toussaint Louverture International Airport in Port-au-Prince.

Haiti is so unlucky! I have a question for you. Who has been your best friend in this life? Whom do you really trust? Who can call you at 10:30 at night, asking for a favor that you know cannot be refused? Whose issues are embedded in your brain? I bet that your answer is the guy that you have played with when you were between 9 and 18 years of age. That's only human. No, it is not only human, birds of a feather flock together. I am not saying that Mom, Dad, or some other family members cannot be that person. So saying, you can't really blame Obama. It's not really his fault. That's part of the streak of Haitian bad luck. We all agree that Haiti's misfortune is directly linked to the country of France. I exposed the links, and the New York Times confirmed that wo years later, in a week-long series of articles in May 2022. But it's not of Haitian doing only. The person that makes all the decisions about Haiti, the United States Secretary of State Antony Blinken, grew up in France. He was there since he was 9 years old. It is only human that he sees Haiti through the eyes of a Frenchman, through the eyes of his old French friends. His brain cannot be wired to understand what Haitians are going through. Whom can the American White House trust to be the best man to take care of Haitian problems than someone that speaks French? That would make him a good choice for America, regarding the management of Haiti. But he might not be so good for Haiti after all. The French thinking is, why did Haiti have to go get its independence? Haiti is getting exactly what it deserves. So, it is not his fault. It is not the fault of the Secretary of State if he cannot understand what is it about that Haiti is crying. So, my friends, don't expect anything to get better in Haiti very soon. The Secretary of State got to be on the side of the French. That's normal. It's just the latest in the streak of bad luck regarding Haiti. And, expect the situation to get worse. It is human nature. If you are Haitian-born and be French at the same time, imagine having spent your infancy in France, and you'll understand.

If the French are really trying and have been successful at keeping Haiti poor, consider the means through which they have managed to get their wish become reality. Here's a good example in the U.S, Secretary of State, among others, unwilling to help the country in the orbit of Uncle Sam.

-Not to be forgotten, the U.S. is one of the five permanent members of the United Nations Security Council, the only UN body with authority to issue resolutions that are binding on member states. To be noted, in alphabetical order they are China, France, Russia, the United Kingdom and the United States.

-The international organizations, using French as a working language include the United Nations, the European Union, UNESCO, NATO, ICC, or International Criminal Court.

-The international organizations headquartered in France: Organization for Economic Cooperation and Development (OECD).

Christine Lagarde, a French politician and diplomat was the president of the European Central Bank, Managing Director of the International Monetary Fund (IMF), French Minister of the Economy, Finance and Industry, just to name a few of the organizations that decide financial decisions regarding other countries, including Haiti. They have money and can use blackmail in dealing with many important people.

France, as indicated, is a powerhouse. And the French have good motive to hurt Haiti. They have entangled Haiti so much that Haitians cannot trust them. They have used so many unimaginable tactics, like the imaginary debt, to hurt Haiti in the past, that they are not worthy of trust. They do not have to say anything at a meeting, their body language will relay the message. They should recuse themselves whenever decisions regarding Haiti are being taken by international organizations.

The United States of America also has a strange relationship with Haiti. They derive their pleasure of their geographic position to Haiti, but still ignore the country.

Geographic phellatio.

THE RELATIONSHIP BETWEEN THE UNITED STATES
AND HAITI IS ONLY PLAYING. NOTHING SERIOUS.

CHAPTER 7

A SAMPLE OF WHAT THE POPULATION IS ENDURING IN HAITI

This is what was in the cards for El Salvador, which turned around on time.

The consequences of this mess now include:

Killing of police officers every day. Torching of police stations frequently. The destruction of public records is epidemic. The justice system cannot function because the files are absent.

Decrease of self-respect; Loss of self-esteem; Decreased respect from others; A constellation of Diseases—Mental illnesses, Mental trauma, Psychosocial problems, Suicide; Dilution of standards; Delinquency; Decrease in education already lacking; Poor performance in governance; Malnutrition; Marasmus; Kwashiorkor, etc. If you are not doing anything to enhance your performance, you are left behind; Loss of will to perform; Lack of fuel; No potable water; No school; No businesses (they are closed); Hospitals cannot care for patients; Pharmacies are torched; Worsening of imported cholera; Unintentional running away from technology of any kind.

These are a fraction of the damage caused by the bandits, whether those in *sapats or kravats* (Creole for those wearing sandals or ties and suited) have done to the nation, to you and your kids, whether those kids are educated abroad or not. Years of sacrifices have been erased. If the peasants do not plant because they cannot sell their crops, the land will remain naked and will be vulnerable to flood and demineralization.

The plantations are disappearing at an alarming rate, because the farmers cannot sell their products. That is a direct consequence of the major national roads and the city streets being blocked by the gangs. Why do we keep destroying things that we cannot replace? The other direct culprit is creeping mistrust, equal to none, leading to lockdowns. As of writing this book, the border with the Dominican Republic is closed. No plane is landing in Haiti, except for the US military that is installing a secret compound at the Toussaint Louverture International Airport in Port-au-Prince. There's no communication with the outside world except for, let us say WhatsApp, if and when the telephone works. The streets are blocked in all directions.

Romantic life in Haiti is almost nonexistent. If you cannot travel, how do you visit your girlfriend? You cannot be in the street after dark, how do you see her. There is no work, the entertainment business is closed completely. No movie theater, no parties, no "kermess or afternoon parties" no *"Fèt chanpèt,"* the peasant fiestas, therefore no celebrations at appropriate time! It is difficult to acquire a condom. There is no safe place to meet a girlfriend unless you live next door. No *"Tap Tap"* for public transportation and no other options. What kind of life is that? Most of the pregnant women are part of some gangs and others are forced to live with a bandit or be raped. The authorities know those who should be punished once justice finally becomes operational. These reluctant mothers have many stories to tell. It's an understatement to say it will take years to repair the damage that has been done.

This is what was about to happen if the bandits and terrorists were not stopped in El Salvador.

Rue des miracles and rue du peuple

Some anecdotal stories of an existence in Haiti. This is what El Salvador escaped.

The other day a preacher reported that an 11-year-old boy who belongs to his church was dead. He asked the crying mother from what kind of sickness? For a young kid doesn't suddenly die like that. The mother replied that the kid had not eaten in three days and died of starvation.

In *Croix-des-Bouquets,* that suburb northeast of Port-au-Prince, at a church function one Sunday, the bandits killed a few parishioners, kidnapped others, including the preacher. They burned all the cars in the parking lot.

At Bel Air/Maya, all the houses in the neighborhood were burned down for no apparent reason. A 90-year-old icon of the neighborhood, and another of 87, who could not run fast enough, were found burned to eschar, as they came out of a corridor in the area.

At Carrefour Feuilles, the bandits went to a moto parking lot, where the moto taxi drivers park their vehicles for safety. They loaded the motos into a big truck and disappeared in the afternoon. An old, non-threatening man, sitting in front of his house, who probably could not even tell what was going on, was executed in his chair, sealing his mouth forever. For no apparent reason, the bandits didn't spare a pregnant woman passing by. She was sacrificed along with her baby.

The expansion of the bandits embraces the takeover of the neighborhoods, the introduction of machine guns and other sophisticated heavy weapons; the exacerbation of the killings; politicians driven away from their homes and seeking refuge in hotels, then moving from hotel to hotel, fearing being killed otherwise. Shooting in the streets, day and night, becomes a pastime. The bandits block the main streets with stolen tractor trailers and charge toll to allow vehicles to pass. And one's car can be burn on the spot, if the driver objects to paying the toll. No one ventures in the street after dark. But even during daylight some streets are not safe. The bandits can seize one's beautiful house turned into their own residence. The only wise decision is to ignore them and flee. Some police officers would be on their payroll. With the deterioration of governance, dangerous things happen all the time.

THE GHOST TOWNS ARE MULTIPLYING

There remains a potential problem in El Salvador. That is why **supporting Haiti should be on their agenda**. The gangs are not silent outside of El Salvador. They are regrouping. How the assault will occur is unknown. The surest bet is that they're planning their comeback. Such powerful groups, with allies elsewhere cannot be eradicated by only one country.

The reason why El Salvador became so important in the talk about Haiti is because the United Nations voted to send Kenya to help Haiti with the issue of insecurity. Though El Salvador has some apparent problems, i.e. thousands of gang members incarcerated, the authorities are accused of having too much power. The president calls himself "cool dictator." To be fair this denomination was expressed because he was accused of having dictatorial tendencies. At the same time 85% of the population reelected him, without any irregularities reported in the electoral process. As stipulated in the constitution, he had vacated the presidency for six months before the vote.

Meanwhile, the Kenyans don't have a better reputation regarding human rights. Granted, I went to El Salvador to witness the changes there, but did not make it to Kenya to have a personal opinion or impression. Whatever I say about Kenya is derived from third party sources.

As per Travel.State.Gov a service of the United States Department of B- Bureau of Consular Affairs themselves the Kenya Travel Advisory is "Do Not Travel". Exercise increase caution in Kenya due to crime, terrorism, civil unrest, and kidnapping. The US Department of State 2023 Country Reports on Human Rights Practices on Kenya reads: Significant human rights issues included credible reports of unlawful or arbitrary killings, including extrajudicial killings; forced disappearance; torture and cases of cruel, inhuman, or degrading treatment of punishment by the government; harsh and life-threatening prison conditions; arbitrary arrest and detention. I still do not see why Kenya can be superior to El Salvador in returning

a country to livable level. It is however the decision of the United States of America and the United Nations in conjunction with CARICOM. I can only give you the facts.

Forgive me to say so, but I think many Haitians would rather have a dictatorial regime instead of having a country ran by uneducated bandits that kill openly with impunity.

CHAPTER 8

HAITIANS, A NEW GENERATION OF "JUIF ERRANT"

When I was growing up, my parents used to talk about *"Juif Errant,"* the "Wandering Jews" who moved from country to country because they didn't have a country of their own. There was even a show staged in Jacmel, the capital of Haiti's southeastern department, called *"Juif errant."* It detailed the difficulties these people faced, moving from one country to the next, to make a living. Now, Haitians are the proverbial "Wandering Jews" of this century. An attestation of this fact is the story of Marie. First, it was an ordeal crossing the border at Ouanaminthe, in Haiti's northeastern region, to get to the Dominican Republic, where she boarded a plane to go to Dominica (La Dominique), another island in the Caribbean. This was planned by a travel agency. By the way, some of these travel agencies make a killing in planning trips for Haitians, and many complaints have been lodged against them.

Back to Marie. From Dominica she was planning to go to St. Thomas. Total cost: $3,000.00. When Haitians from Guadeloupe came to board to go also to St. Thomas, the price was jacked up to $4,000.00. They could not come up with the money. Kockey, the fixer, made them work on his plantain plantations for a year. They finally had a planned day to go to St. Thomas on a boat originating from St. Martin. The ship that was supposed to pick them up in Dominica to take them to St. Thomas was a no show, because the stingy fixer did not pay enough of the money. It appears that Kockey collected $4,000 from each person and was paying the ship $1000 per head. That is on top having charged the travelers $100 every month for rent. Those people had to get money from family back home, or from those in the diaspora to meet the balance. Kockey's business was flourishing, whatnot with multiple houses he owned and renting rooms to Haitians, several in one room. Instead of doing business with the ship owner as planned, he went to Roseau and rented a small boat for the transportation. He tried to crowd 35 people in a boat fitted for 25. The boat capsized. People were dying as the boat was sinking. My friend was saved by someone who had a crush on her. Al, his name, knew how to swim and was able to save Marie. There was an understanding between Marie and Al for after they reach their destination. They will begin a boyfriend/girlfriend relationship. Incidentally, they were all arrested by the police.

Here for another story about another modern wandering Haitian called Lolo. It started with a trip to Brazil. His family helped him make the trip, by arranging to have him travel from Aquin, in Haiti's southern region, to Port-au-Prince, the capital, to obtain his passport. He was stopped by a gang in the street. They mistook him from belonging to a rival gang. But they let him go when they realized that he was indeed from Aquin. After multiple trips from Ste. Thérèse in Pétion-Ville to Carrefour without any success in getting the passport, and after losing money to people that promised and never delivered, he went back to Aquin with an empty pocket. Finally, he got the passport in Aquin, after a three-month wait. He applied for a Brazilian visa that took another three months. Finally, he made it to Brazil, where he was making enough just to eat. He could not save any money in Sao Paulo. He also could not send money to family back home, for he had to pay back money he borrowed to go to Brazil. Then, he decided to risk his life and make the trip from Brazil to the United States of America. He said that he had to go through Argentine and Bolivia, but that doesn't make much sense, because those countries are to the south of Brazil. He was heading north. Only he knows what he went through. I will take his word for it. Hundreds of Haitians attempted the same trip. Sometimes they would spend three days sitting in a bus. Some of his comrades, he said, had developed swollen legs, some passed out along the way. There was no time for a hospital visit. They just washed their faces and kept going.

With all the money these people spent in search of El Dorado, one asks why couldn't they open a business and stay back home? Apparently Hope is a better draw than taking a chance at home, where success is so slim, and gang activities aplenty! In that light, staying home is not worth it. The other reason is that, while the family loves you and would help when in danger, they are not disposed to help one invest in the country anymore, because failure is a safe bet.

Haitians looking for a life abroad have made a lot of other people rich. The amount of money spent by Haitians passing though countries to get to the United States is humongous. They are charged fees that do not exist. They must pay at every step of their trip to the southern border of the United States. The Police officers collect "pedi-toll" foot (toll) for themselves, and their commanders are numerous stopping points. For, they are charged in every city they cross or reach. When they cross the border to another country in their dangerous trip, they have to start the process all over again. Sometimes they are dilapidated and have to call back home to ask for more money that no one back home has anymore. Consider that these people have sold their cattle, their land and everything else at a great discount to be able to get to where they are. Thus, sometimes, they resort to selling of themselves to get to the next step. One would think that depressed as these people are by this time, they would commit suicide. On the contrary, resilient as ever, they often show the best of their humanness. For them it becomes a war for life itself. They fight until they stop breathing or arrive at their destination.

Jina was already living in Santo Domingo. She was stable. She was no longer looking for a job. She had her own business, selling dresses. It was not great, but it was good enough to make a living. But that was not enough for her. She was still looking for greener pastures. She sold her business and decided to go to the United States. It was a long trip that called for boarding multiple buses, from Santo Domingo to Ouanaminthe. And the bridge at the border was closed, because of a dispute between the Dominican Republic and Haiti regarding a canal that Haitians were building to access water on the Massacre River. The Dominican President was so upset that he deployed the Army and Air Force to the border to intimidate Haiti. Finally, he decided to open the gate every noon to let people out. Jina crossed the border and went to Cap-Haitian. She was staying with a friend that was not thrilled to shelter her. She had to leave and go to Port-au-Prince, where she found a place to live at the Fontamara neighborhood. She found a travel agency. She got her papers, including passport and the yellow card to go to Nicaragua. One morning, at 11 o'clock, she landed in Nicaragua, took a bus, paying $50, and in six (6) hours, she reached Honduras. She continued on to the Guatemala border, but the Guatemalan border was closed when she arrived. She slept on the floor, waiting for the border to open. In Guatemala, she was taken aside and despoiled of her valuables by the authorities. She had to call Haiti for more money to continue the trip. When the money arrived, she paid a "passer" or "guide" who took her through the mountainous region, walking during three (3) days to reach the state of Tabasco in Mexico. There was no way to take pictures. First you have to stay focused, second, if you stop to take pictures, you have to play catchup. There were dead people by the side of the road. One couldn't afford to feel pity for them, because if one loses focus, there's the possibility of being next. The "rack or jungle" is the most difficult path of the trip. That is where most people lose their lives. The jungle between Colombia and Panama is the most dangerous of all. She did not have to go through that one. The walk continued a few days and nights to Juchitan, in the state of Oaxaca. That is where one had to buy a bus ticket to go to Mexico City. The bus station was packed with migrants from all over the world. She was there three (3) days and could not get a ticket. She gave someone 1,500 pesos to help her get a ticket. The money was stolen. She spoke to one of the bus drivers that had pity on her and accepted to let her in his bus for 1500 pesos without a ticket. She was finally on her way to Mexico City. It was not an easy trip, but she made it. Now in Mexico City she spent the first night in front of a house in town. A passerby offered to get her a room the second night. They were six (6) in the room for 1000 pesos a head. The Mexico City stay lasted three (3) months. It was cold and muggy. These feelings are amplified, she said, when one doesn't have the proper clothing. Remember that one cannot afford a blanket which costs quite a bit, while already paying right and left for all sorts of things, just to have an appearance of the right to be in someone else's country. She finally could file on the CBP site (US Custom and Border Protection), a branch of the US Department of Homeland Security. Every day she had to check the site to see if her team of 52 people was given an authorization to enter the United States. Some teams had 150 people. Some people put their names in two (2) different teams. Automatically, that cancelled the second team. The day she received the positive message from CPB was the happiest of her life, a happiness that soon faded away, because of the way she was received by her family here in "America."

Ti Joseph recounted a story of when he was coming to the United States in a wooden 20-foot boat with 20 people on board. People were stacked up like sardines in a can. One could not move much during the whole trip. There was no wind, still there was problem with the boat taking water, it was like a real flood. That was exacerbated by the weight of the passengers. The bouncer had no choice but to throw some people overboard to save the ones that remained. Besides, the sharks were circling around the boat, they had to be fed, otherwise they would destroy the boat. After all these sacrifices, the boat was stopped by the Coast Guard and everyone was returned to Haiti.

By JAMES WAH
DEFYING ALL LAWS OF PHYSICS AND NATURE,
HAITIANS TRAVELLING TO THE US.

It is true that Haitians have to use the help of our neighbors, but it is a one-sided friendship. A lot of Haitians closed their business and reopened them in the Dominican Republic. I can understand, because they are running away from hell. As it's said in Haiti, "It's running away from the rain and falling into the deep river." From what I hear, it is hell-on-earth on the other side of the island, just because you are Haitian. A case in point is Pierre, a Haitian- born American citizen, who was in Haiti when the border was closed, due to the fight over the canal construction, as previously mentioned. It should be noted that the Dominican Republic has a dozen canals accessing water on the Massacre River, and the president of the Republic next door started the ornery dispute when the Haitians began building the first canal to the river serving as border between the two countries for a few miles. The Dominican government sent army units to the border to intimidate the Haitians, to no avail. The Creole slogan *"Kanal la p ap kanpe,"* (There's no stopping building the canal) became a rallying cry. The whole episode affected Pierre's plan to fly from Haiti to the U.S. As an American citizen, eventually he was allowed to cross the border. When he arrived at the airport, they forced him to pay $1,800.00 in order to let him board his flight. They told him that he would miss his plane and will have to buy another emergency ticket if there's any delay in payment. He had to pay a total of almost $2,000 to go back home in the U.S.

Francky a Haitian-born American citizen, non-Spanish speaking, was in Santo Domingo. He liked it and overstayed three (3) months. On his way back to the U.S. he was charged a hefty fine for every month he overstayed. He spoke to the supervisor who was understanding and waved the fine. The officer who was supposed to stamp the passport refused to comply. The supervisor was contacted again. The reason she refused to obey a direct order is because it had to do with a Haitian. The supervisor told her that he has an American passport. Though she stamped the passport, she kept saying to her co-workers that he should pay because he was born in Haiti.

In February I made a trip to the Mexican and American border by McAllen and Reynosa. The condition Haitians are living is far from being desirable, but it is still better than in Haiti ravaged by a war without purpose. A war whose purpose is unknown to all of us. That got to make it difficult to end. Haitians are suffering everywhere. Some of these stories would make you cry like if you had lost something personally. I will spare you those.

I would ask why but I know that Haiti had to pay for kicking the bottom of the colons. Haiti had to pay for being the crib of freedom. Haiti had to pay for freeing the Dominican Republic. Haiti had to pay for freeing South America. Haiti had to pay for costing big countries

HAITI, CRUEL AND UNUSUAL PUNISHMENT

a large loss of income. Haiti had to pay because the Europeans lost their prestigious position of being superior to other races. But wait a minute a minute, Haiti paid. Yes, Haiti paid what a country 354 times its size could not pay. (USA) 37967437 square miles divided by (Haiti) 10714 square miles = 354 times. Still, Haiti cannot look ahead because it is blinded. There are a lot of anecdotal stories of Haitian suffering everywhere. I sincerely do not know when this is going to get better.

There are many anecdotal stories regarding Haitians suffering everywhere because of their origin, I sincerely don't know when this will get better or end totally.

CHAPTER 9

WHAT ARE HAITI'S OPTIONS?

How to end this nightmare, once and for all? There have been a lot of conflicts in the world. Most of the time when they last it is because people are not realistic. The longer they last the more irreparable damage has been made. Most importantly one should carefully estimate the potential gains and losses of a concession. Loss of life and preparation of the next generation are the most important considerations in these debates. Remember that no one wins when disastrous situations last. If the conflict continues, everyone loses something.

Often, it' after losing everything that people realize that they should have or could have made a deal much earlier and come out ahead. So, be careful!

Let us see what are available for Haiti to come out of this conjuncture.

1. OVERPOWER THE GANGS. You, I am addressing the government, can try to reduce them to submission. However, you'll need more manpower, more and better weapons that you don't have. You cannot afford to underestimate the terrorists. They have been doing this for a long time. Definitely, they have acquired some experience. They also have a silent army behind them, one that I call *"Criminals under cover."* They are the cousins, the mothers,

the aunties or friends who are not part of the gangs, but would not mind being on the lookout for them. They are the friends who are well aware of the crimes being committed by the bandits, but won't tell them to stop, because they are afraid of reprisals or of losing the benefits of the money that will stop coming. Also, there's no way ignoring the bandits within. These are the people working with and for the justice system who notify the bandits whenever an attack is imminent, thus undermining the element of surprise. You may get an outside army to, eventually, dominate them, but you don't have the money to keep that going. Let's say you build your own army. You'll need to keep watch for the traitors that will be on board. The bandits will try vigorously to infiltrate the army. They will try to undermine your work. The bandits also will attack the training camp of your future soldiers. They will do so repeatedly in order to prevent you from succeeding in your preparation. And you still will need more money. You can employ youngsters with a promissory note like an "I owe you". The money will come when the security is established. You will need an army of at least 50,000 to 80,000 men to control the gangs. There's the temptation of turning to foreign armies, but most are not really interested in dying for you, no matter the amount you're ready to disburse for their help. They have no interest in your country, they're only there on a limited mandate, then they're gone. Another problem is that every time an outside power comes to Haiti it is a bad experience, invariably they leave a bad taste in our mouth. When they leave the country, no one knows what they took away with them. What they leave is often very detrimental to the people, such as communicable diseases and fatherless children. Moreover, they can leave sleeper cells that will cause turmoil and easily overthrow the government on demand. This is a well-known technic. And there's no forgetting that we have to deal also with the suited and bandits wearing cravatsc, who are really the decision makers who furnish the weapons to the sandal wearing bandits.

Looking at all aspects of banditry, one will need a large sum of money to finance an eventual army and have the capacity to post armed soldiers at every street corner. Consider that El Salvador, which has half the population of Haiti, spent between $500 and $600 million to stabilize their country.

2.   MAKE A DEAL WITH THE DEVIL. The advantage of amnesty is that the bandits could put their arms down right now and immediately we can start with our normal lives. Instead of a continuous war that lingers for 10 or more years, during which thousands of deaths are registered, accompanied with destruction of infrastructure and homes. Who wants that when one can start enjoying some peaceful time immediately. It has been done elsewhere, such as in Colombia, South America.

In Haiti the bandits have been asking for amnesty but continue to carry on with their atrociously horrible mission. There is nothing serious in the air. When a young American missionary couple was murdered in an orphanage, the situation in Haiti turned into a totally different ballgame. This might give the United States the pretext to officially declare war on the bandits in Haiti. It's worth noting that, in general, the American public usually supports the government when an American is killed overseas.

In Colombia, for example, the amnesty has worked. Colombia was dealing with the "FARC Rebels," or *Fuerzas Armadas Revolucionarias de Colombia*. They laid down their arms after 52 years of fighting and destruction, having kept the country in continuous insecurity, with mental illness taking a toll, on top of rape of the female population, no age spared, the indiscriminate killing, infrastructure destruction, deforestation and illegal mining. Worse yet, with the absence of education and of health care, ignorance set in, leading to complete backwardness and a general absence of trust. Then, there was the historic peace agreement, in 2016, when most of the guerrillas laid down their arms. And according to published statistics, up to 2022, the annual GDP of Colombia has been as high as 7.3%.

The terrorists, bandits, assassins, anarchists, robbers, muggers, outlaws or whatever we want to call them were divided into several categories: minor criminals or junior members of the gangs and the real actors called heads of gangs or close affiliates.

During the transitioning from war to peace, some former fighters were targeted in revenge killings triggered by bitterness about the many massacres carried out by the terrorists. That couldn't be prevented. Based on common sense, the bandits will be aware that this is a possibility in Haiti also, something underlying their reluctance in making peace. In fact, in Haiti, a movement of **Bwa Kale,** by the population, taking justice into their hands, has already led to gross execution of some bandits.

Some of the bandits are also going to be bitter because of loss of power. Some arms and ammunition are not going to be tendered to the authorities, something that needs to be dealt with in advance.

The bandits will need to be reprogrammed.

There will be a void if the army is not reinstated fully.

There will be division among the former bandits, with some of them proceeding to rearm themselves and sabotage any peace process.

Therefore, a serious commission should be set up to oversee the return of former gang members to civilian life.

There will be a need for army and/or police units maintaining strict surveillance in areas where former bandits are being reintegrated into civilian life.

The bandits must declare all their assets and hand them over. The money amassed from their depredations will be used in reconstruction projects of the country.

The bandits will have to report and document drug dealings and their atrocities.

Amnesty might seem too lenient, but the option is a continuous war that we will not be able to handle. For example, according to United Nations statistics, in 2023 there were 4,789 killings in Haiti, 110% higher than in 2022.

3. THIS IS ANOTHER POTENTIAL OPTION FOR HAITI. Pay the bandits for their guns and rehabilitate them. As it is, most of the bandits, despite collecting money from their victims all over the country, look like people that can't afford a t-shirt or a pair of decent rubber flippers. They don't appear as if they've spent $10 on what they wear. If they're offered $100 in U.S. currency for their guns, they could readily give up the guns and, for the first time in a long time, enjoy a good meal. Of course, there are potential reasons why they may not accept such a proposal: There is an aura of power attached to holding a gun on someone unable to use self-defense; the $100 offered them is temporary, while the power of the gun appears eternal, even if there is no ammunition, but no one knows that the gun could be empty; there's fear of reprisals from other gang members; and the bandits could be afraid of the unknown, thinking that on giving up their weapons, that wouldn't prevent the justice system from coming after them!

4. THE QUESTION REMAINS REGARDNGING THE ORIGIN OF THE GUNS. Where did the expensive assault weapons originate and who was supplying them to the bandits? Undeniably, it's been widely reported that the arms come from Miami and the Dominican Republic. If so, how did they escape

surveillance of the American and Dominican authorities? What interest does the American government or any entity in Haiti has in arming uneducated individuals having little to lose? These are people that have been already brainwashed to hate the haves (with or without reason). Did their patrons expect they would be able to control their minions after they've acquired the power of holding those guns? Had the gun providers ever thought that some smart ones among the bandits could try to take control of the situation once they had enough guns?

5. OTER UNANSWERED QUESTIONS: Why did the bandits have to kick people out of their homes in a whole neighborhood if they did not need the houses or what was in them? Let us assume that they needed control of the whole neighborhood, for usually they do nothing with the dwellings after they've been vacated. If it's the neighborhoods they needed, what are they waiting for before taking them over? We fail to understand this erratic behavior. We have yet to decipher the puzzle, but it's fair to say that their plan is not terminated,

The potential for a dangerous future exists, if the gangs are not destroyed completely. They must be eradicated. This makes me think about the perspicacity of Ambassador Raymond Joseph, who's given me a hand in editing this book. On September 8, 2021, after gangs had seized the Port-au-Prince southern suburb of Martissant, on June 1st of that year, he had launched a slogan in Creole in the Haiti-Observateur, which he often repeated: *"Toutotan kesyon gang nan pa regle, anyen pa ka regle ann Ayiti!"* (As long as the gang issue isn't resolved, nothing can be resolved in Haiti.)

Martissant, on National Route No.2, is the gateway to Haiti's Greater southern region, thus since that time, traffic has been greatly restricted between the capital and four of the country's 10 departments, as the mini-states are called. And the isolation of the capital was completed, when the gangs took control of National Route No. 1, to the Greater northern region with four departments and also Route No. 3, connecting Port-au-Prince with the Central Plateau and the eastern region leading to the border with the Dominican Republic.

Meanwhile, the bandits have been collecting money from kidnapping, requesting payment of millions of US dollars. Someone in these groups must have accumulated a fortune. In an election, usually the one that has the money is the one that wins. If the bandits are able to infiltrate the executive, the legislative and the judicial, we are all cooked. No one will be able to stop them. Of course, there is someone that can stop them but that someone might not have any interest in Haiti. Any group not under gang control will be afraid to participate in any vote. They will be intimidated by the bandits. The ones with the guns are the ones who will secure the votes. So, we warned all about the upcoming elections.

Gangs are becoming more powerful all over the Americas. Very rich, they operate in silence. They got increasingly aggressive in Mexico, where sixty politicians were assassinated before the election of June 2024.

If the bandits are able to kill their opponents, if they can buy power, if they can buy and intimidate the media, they have already won. In such a situation, what will stop them from interfering in the elections of other countries, such as Haiti. If their threat isn't soon addressed, these powerful organizations are poised to act, and sad to say, from their starting position, the next 25 to 50 years will be in their hands.

We have the laws; They must be applied in their cases. We can't allow to close our eyes on what some of our friends do, as often happens. For their actions are not only wrong, but extremely dangerous.

We also need to use our influence in inducing a change in the mentality of the population. It's not an easy task, when you take into consideration that some people who have a decent job in the United States are dying to get a job in Haiti. Why so? Because they don't have to show up for work, yet get paid regularly, even if the job pays only 20% of what was being made in the U.S. But, there's a secret to it. Money can be made on the side with that job. I ask: Can we do the right thing by Haiti? For, following the rules, Haiti can no longer do anything for you. And I put the question to all: What have you done for Haiti lately?

CHAPTER 10

WHY CAN'T HAITIANS DO IT TOO?

I understand that Haiti is a financial amputee, but Haitians must stop begging. If you are begging, you are inviting people to ask you what's going on. You also are inviting them to give you advice. That might not stop there. Sometimes it goes as far as your financier imposing rules, such as how the money you're being given will be spent. Do not ask yourself why so many other people are meddling in your business. Your business is not really yours, if the money spent is not entirely yours.

We have not been able to do it, because those in power, the politicians, don't seem to have any interest in doing what must be done. Intoxicated by power and corrupted to the core, they may realize what they should have done only after they are deprived both of power and the privileges thereof.

The element of greed is really overwhelming in Haiti. Some people have made so much money that some of it is coming out of all the orifices of their body. Yet, they keep acting as if they don't have enough. Moreover, impunity being the rule, they goad you, as if saying: "If you can, just touch me!"

The people who, behind the scene, are really in charge of what's happening, prevent the politicians to act in the interest of the people. And they go along with the game because they enjoy the perks derived from power. How did we get there? The answer is the same as in El Salvador in the last few years. We got there because of Haitian mismanagement. We got some aid from France, the United States and Canada. Defending their own interests, they close their eyes, or in certain cases, become silent enablers of the mayhem.

CHAPTER 11

LET US SPECULATE

It sounds and looks like the death of Jovenel Moïse Haiti's president killed in the bedroom of his highly secured residence, was strategic. It was planned for sure but the people that did it may not have known for sure what they were doing. So far, it looks as if with so many people involved, several goals were intended, perhaps even some conflicting. Is it coincidental that the president never held an election, causing lack of democratic representation in Haiti? Is it by chance that the Upper and Lower chambers of Parliament were emptied? That, to me gives the impression that someone wanted unrestrained power for the Prime Minister, who disposed of carte blanche regarding decisions he would make. Could the de facto Prime Minister Ariel Henry, who replaced President Moïse, be an ally of another power? To be remembered, he was educated in Montpellier, France. The president might have taught that it was going to help him. He might have been advised that it would be good to accomplish what he intended to do. It seems that his advisers led him to believe it was good for him, but he did not know his life was part of the plan. Then, he was assassinated a day before the installation of the Prime Minister. Could 11 million people plus the diaspora have been blinded and cannot see that strategy? Was the release of prisoners in two major penitentiaries also coincidental? The assassins of a president are released from prison by a gang of bandits! Coincidental? These are really weird acts.

Prime Minister Gérard Latortue, who was named to his post in 2004, was a high cadre of the United Nations. His first move, after his nomination, was to travel to France to declare that the claim of $21 billion in reparations to Haiti, by France demanded by President Aristide is stupidity. As far as I am concerned, I want to give credit to anyone who tries to help Haiti. After a declaration like that, can one wonder if Mr. Latortue had signed any paper annulling the official claim of restitution by President Aristide?

By SILENT ARTIST
PRIME MINISTER GERARD LATORTUE SHAKING HANDS WITH PRESIDENT JACQUES CHIRAC. PRESIDENT ARISTIDE IS MUTED,

The current Prime Minister of Haiti, Dr. Garry Conille, is very promising in the eyes of many Haitians. Having been another high UN cadre. He is aware of the UN's modus operandi. He is known by them, just as he knows them. They meet in the hallways, they go to the same parties, they have each other's special phone numbers. Could his nomination have been dictated by the UN? Has there been any deal made? This would be the second time that a high UN cadre is managing Haiti. It could be a good thing, just as it could also be bad. Let us wait and see what will happen.

CHAPTER 12

WE WILL MAKE IT SIMPLE

We can talk about reparations or restitution. There is no difference to anyone who has been able to calculate the monetary damage to Haiti. Anyone who steals a property at gun point is considered an outlaw in any society. But, as it is, certain countries can do it freely in the case of weaker countries, with impunity.

Haitian culture has been decimated. Cultural events are at a standstill. This was not experienced even during the Holocaust. The Jews found a way to interact during the Nazi era, but Haitians cannot get out of their houses to freely participate in some events and performance of certain ceremonies.

For the pleasure of your majesty, you reading this, I will repeat the calculation I already made in my last book.

To explain the damage caused to Haiti by France, let me introduce some math/facts. Before I get into that, I'll point out that Haitians talk about damage, while for the French it is well-deserved punishment.

On April 30, 1803 the United States of America paid $5.25 per square kilometer, according to a bac-dated document for the Louisiana Purchase, a total of 50,000,000.00 francs.

At conversion exchange rate of 4.4444 francs for a dollar, the purchase amounted to $11,250,000.00.

Surface area: 2,140,000 square kilometers.
Unit price: $5.25/square kilometer. $5.25

March 30, 1867, the United States of America paid $4.19 per square kilometer in another deal:

The Alaska purchase: $7,200,000.00
Surface area: 1,717,855 square kilometers
Unit price: $4.19/square kilometer. $4.19

In 1825 Haiti paid an indemnity, at gun point, of $1216.22 per square kilometer. In 1838 the indemnity was reduced to 90 million gold francs, but a dollar spent by Haiti was $2 because of a 50% tax imposed by France.

Surface area: 27,750 square kilometers.
Conversion exchange rate: $4.4444 francs for a dollar.
Reduced indemnity in dollars: $40,500,405.00
Unit price: $1,459.47/square kilometer. $1,459.47

Meaning:
Louisiana purchase $5.25 / Km2
Alaska purchase $4.19 / Km2
Haiti indemnity $1,459.47/ Km2

We are using the reduced indemnity to show how horribly wrong the treatment was.

CHAPTER 13

HAITI HAS BEEN IMPOVERISHED

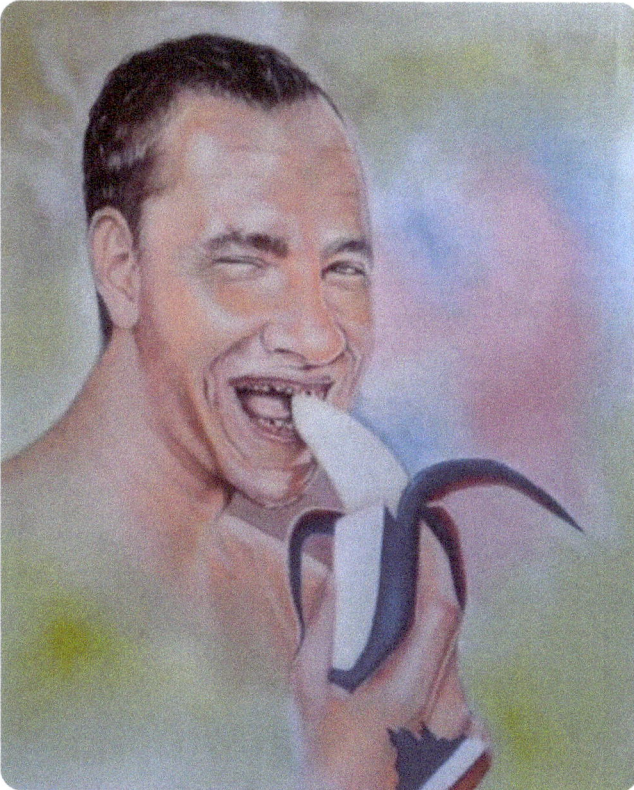

By ISMAEL ST. LOUIS
"ROTTEN TEETH ARE STRONGER ON BANANA" or
MIGHT MAKES RIGHT

You break it, you fix it. The Eiffel Tower was built with Haitian money and sweat. It belongs to Haitians. No one checked what happened to Haiti, because everyone assumed Blacks to be incompetent. The decadence was believed to be a direct, 100 percent (100%) consequence of Haitians' doing. I know what happened, it just didn't happen of itself and overnight. No, Haiti did not just become the poorest country of the Western Hemisphere. Haiti was engineered to be poor. Haiti's poverty was manufactured. The way Haiti is right now, is not coincidental. This is the way Haiti was planned to be. Saying so is not an excuse for the Haitian traitors that have sold out the country.

France's predatory practices toward Haiti are continuing till today and must stop. Haiti deserves congratulations. How did that country manage to pay that exorbitant amount of money? Even if Haiti economy was the size of that of the United States, it would have a hard time recovering. To pay $1,459.44 for a square kilometer of land that is worth $5.25 or less is incomprehensible and unbelievable.

To use the same calculation the French used to make Haitians pay at gunpoint:

Paying $1,459.44 for a unit of land that America paid $5.25 for is like buying:

One gallon of whole milk of $3.97 for **$1,103.58**
A dozen Grade A eggs of $4.93 for **$1,370.44**
Your Honda Accord of $29,060.00 for **$8,078,098.80.**
that is 8 million dollars.
An average US condo of 200,000.00 for **$ 55,596,000.00**

That is a colossal $55,596,000.00 dollars if you pay cash. Your down payment of 20% would be ($11,119,200.00) or 55 times the real value of the condo. Please forget about the monthly payments. Keep in mind that the indemnity was paid over 122 years, at 5 % interest. Imagine paying interest on a condo for 122 years or 4+ generations. This is just not imaginable. **That is not even counting the fees and interests charged by the French banks that I call** *poignard, a* **dagger.**

The first payment was 24 million francs. This is an amount that the United States had great difficulty paying for the Louisiana Purchase. That is almost the amount of money paid by the United States to France for fifteen states today: Arkansas, Colorado, Iowa, Kansas, Louisiana, Oklahoma, Minnesota, Missouri, Montana, Nebraska, New Mexico, North Dakota, South Dakota, Texas, and Wyoming. Since Haiti didn't have any money to pay the first payment, the country had to borrow money from Fench banks to pay France. What an abomination to all mankind!

If the United States of America had to pay the same price per square kilometer to France, the Louisiana Purchase would have been $3,127,275,000.00 (3.1 billion) instead of $11.25 million. That is a colossal 277.98 times the value of the land. There is no name for this other than extortion, robbery or plain hold-up. That is criminal. Remember that we did not have to pay anything. We won the war on the battlefield, on November 18, 1803. We did not owe France anything, *zip, zero, zilch, nada!*

The amount of the indemnity was 3.6 times the Louisiana Purchase (180 million francs (or 90 million x 2) as opposed to 50 million francs). Calculated in 2017, the value of the Louisiana Purchase was equivalent to $600 billion in American currency. If we multiply that by 3.6 that would make the value of indemnity 2,160 billion American dollars or more than two (2) trillion American dollars. Way to go, France! The interests are not included. This is where Haiti's money went. I don't think a cash cow could have been used to milk more money than that.

ANOTHER INTERESTING CALCULATION:

THE REDUCED INDEMNITY: $40,500,405.00
POPULATION AT INDEPENDENCE: 500,000 SLAVES + 24,000
MULATTOS = 524,000

$40,500,405/ 524,000 INHABITANTS = $77.29 PAID PER
IHABITANT.

Price of a Km2 of land in the USA= $5.25

$77.29/ $5.25 = 14 KM2 OWED PER INABITANT IN HAITI, MNJ

Haiti paid France the value of 14 X 524,000 = 7,3360,000 square
kilometers for a country with a surface area of only 27,750 square
kilometers.

No matter how it's sliced, this was a huge amount of money.

Based on common sense, something did not sound good with that deal.
In fact, it was not a deal, it was a **HOLDUP**, according to the New
York Times. France knows how to protect its interests. Remember that
Haiti declared itself a free land and was providing citizenship to all
foreigners who arrived on its shores, including nonwhites. **Haiti had to
be stopped**. Do you think that the colonists would accept that their boat
full of slaves be diverted to Haiti where the slaves were given freedom
on the spot? They dried up all the potential revenues of the country.
Haiti remained bankrupt since that artificial independence. Haiti was
placed in a situation that no other country placed in a similar situation
would be able to survive such assault. This is worse than the Holocaust,
or dropping a nuclear bomb, and a hydrogen bomb combined. Thus was
Haiti made to be an example for all who wanted and fought to be free
from slavery.

Slavery was abolished in the United States in 1863. France abolished slavery on paper in 1794. Why was Haiti paying for a "loss of slaves" until 1947? Why did Haiti have to pay an exorbitant amount of money when the "debtor" themselves had been calling slavery illegal for 153 years?

There was no money exchanged for loss of slaves when the USA became independent of England. Besides, France built an expensive monument to congratulate the Americans for their independence. It is called Lady Liberty, that Statue at Liberty Island in the harbor of New York City. Irony or hypocrisy?

Make of this what you want. I am just reporting the facts.

Haiti did not have a chance. This move by France was foolproof and well calculated. Even if the plan failed, they had so much to gain that it was still a win-win situation for them. Haiti was DOA (dead on arrival). Because CPR (cardiopulmonary resuscitation) was progressing for 198 years, starting on the date the indemnity was signed in 1825. Innocently, we believed the patient was alive. That was a big mistake. **This situation made Haitians experience the ugliest side of human beings**.

I don't hate French people. I have French friends that I value and love. I just hate the treatment of my former motherland by theirs. Now I am saying it out loud: *"Slavery is not coming back. Give the country a break."*

To be noted, there was no mention of loss of slaves during the discussions about the Louisiana Purchase. This is a bombshell, because Haiti's indemnity was more for loss of slaves, making it supposedly more expensive and condescending.

THE UNITED STATES OF AMERICA DID NOT HAVE TO PAY FOR LOSS OF SLAVES, FOR THE LOUISIANA PURCHASE, NOR FOR THEIR INDEPENDENCE FROM ENGLAND.

Every problem has a solution, If you don't look for it, it will not look for you.

HERE IS OUR LIST OF POTENTIAL SOLUTIONS FOR HAITI.

PAINTING by JAMES CESAR WAH
THE EIFFEL TOWER COULD HAVE BEEN "CITE SOLEY"
OF HAITI INSTEAD OF THE SLUM THAT IT IS NOW.

Where is the money going to come from for restitution to Haiti?

There is no doubt anymore that part of the indemnity money built the Eiffel Tower, the most valuable monument in Europe that **every Haitian should be proud to have made the construction possible.**

France will say the country doesn't have money for that. The 245 million euros that the Eiffel Tower makes every year are not the only income that the Eiffel Tower brings to France. To this we can add some significant economic contributions in the **hospitality** business, in **restaurants, transportation, car rental, entertainment, sports, museum visits, et all.** All that gives a significant boost to the economy of France. **The Eiffel Tower is now worth more than 500 billion euros. A loan of 200 billion euros on the Tower to repay Haiti could easily solve the problem and would certainly help Haiti. Getting 40% back is better than a complete loss.**

Things are so bad that the important institution that is the New York Times didn't cringe in its revisit of the "double debt" imposed on Haiti in a week-long series of articles in May 2022. Remember that the government of President Macron had said that they could not comment on the articles, because France was in the process of "changing government". As of writing, it has been three years since that statement. Changing that government is an impossible task because it is still the same government that was reelected. That means we are never going to have an answer.

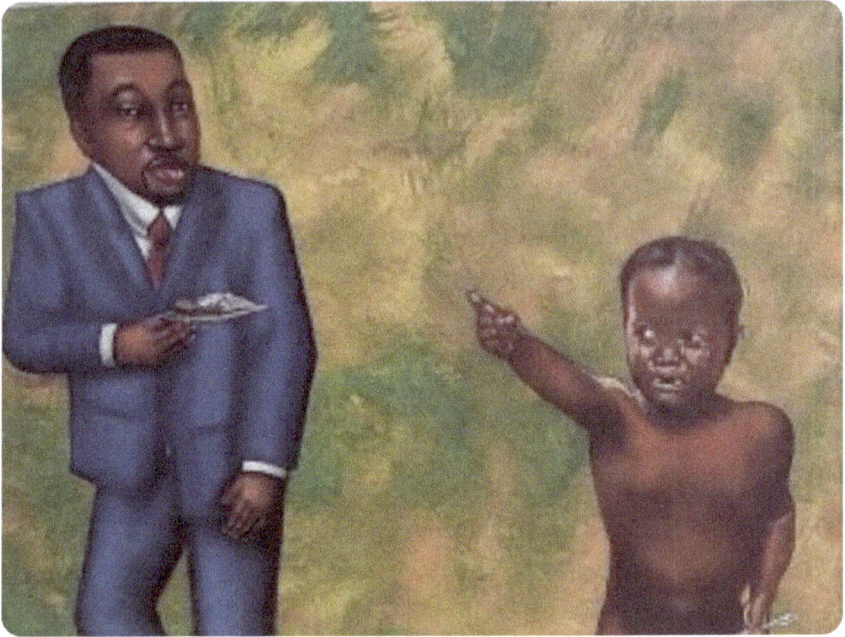

PAINTING by SILENT ARTIST
"THAT" SUMMARIZED IT ALL

CHAPTER 14

LEGALITY OR LEGITIMACY OF THE INDEMNITY

The information below is more elaborate in two previous books: *"Gerard Germain, The Luckiest Man Who Grew Up In An Engineered and Manufactured Poverty"* and in *"Eiffel Tower, Pride of Haiti."*

The law in the 1800 voided any contract between a white and a non-white. It was illegal for the slaves (black) to sign the indemnity (contract) with France (white). It was illegal for the slaves to enter into contract with France. Legally, there was no deal between Haiti and France, based on their own international law in force then. The indemnity is, therefore, null, inadmissible, and void. The indemnity is unjustified.

Slavery was abolished –on paper—by France in 1794 and by the United States in 1863. Why was Haiti paying for "loss of slaves" until 1947?

Since Jean Pierre Boyer, who signed the document recognizing Haiti's debt to France, was the son of a Frenchman, obviously there is conflict of interest. Moreover, that's proven when, later, Jean Pierre

Boyer chose to be exiled in France. He should not have been signing for Haiti.

The whole island of Haiti signed the indemnity. At the time Haiti and the Dominican Republic were one country, with one president: Jean Pierre Boyer. Haiti ended up occupying one-third of the landmass and kept paying the debt, while the Dominican Republic, extended on two-thirds of the island, didn't pay a penny, and brags on how good it is compared to Haiti. If France shared some of the money of the indemnity with Spain, which had lost its Dominican colony, the papers regarding that have been lost or are hidden somewhere.

The Haitian officials, who engineered a sweetheart deal favorable for a bank in France later retired there. Meanwhile, everything that happened between France and Haiti, including slavery and indemnity, remains a secret in France.

The loser of a war is generally the one that pays. Why did the winner, in this case Haiti, had to pay? That never happened in the history of mankind. No precedent can be found.

The indemnity was paid at gunpoint. But it's a well-known fact that if a Toy Gun is used in a hold-up, the aggressor ends up going to jail. Why is it okay for a rich country to do it with real guns, in fact with gunboats, to a poor country and still reaping honors all around? In an analysis, dated October 5, 2021, an NPR headline dubs it "The Greatest Heist in History."

CHAPTER 15

A PLAN FOR SELF-SUFFICIENCY IN 5 YEARS.

1. **Resolve the insecurity issue once and for all.** That will open the country and help with rampant poverty. The diaspora will come in with money. We can have tourists again. Anyone found destroying the country's plan will be severely punished. Through a public campaign, they will be made aware of the consequences of their actions.

   Let us plan to go from 60% below the poverty line to 10%, leading to improvement in unemployment, crime and social unrest.

2. **Education again and again.** We need to educate the population at all levels. Health care cannot come before education. We are four years behind in the education that we had in the past, though it was already quite lacking in substance.

3. **Close the country for two years, give the population a crash course in English or Spanish.** Teach everyone how to read. We really need to work harder on alphabetization. We already have a head start. With the advent of computers, smartphones, reading and writing have had a boost, with texting gaining in popularity.

Definitely, literacy is improving. Unfortunately, Haiti is hampered linguistically, as a Creole speaking country. We should get Haitians to be literate in the languages I have mentioned, surrounded as we are by English- and Spanish-speaking countries. Still, not being educated doesn't mean one is dumb. I know people who don't know how to read and write, but who make calculations that are unimaginable for someone who never set foot in a school. For example, it's amazing watching the illiterate merchants at the open markets counting their money. How do you think analphabets count money into the billion, trillion, and quadrillion in Zimbabwe? I am, therefore, certain that technology is going to make a dent in analphabetism. But, as stated above, I maintain that the country needs a crash course in reading and writing. Many Americans and Haitians would happily come to a post-gang Haiti to teach, even for free. We need to increase education in rural Haiti to increase opportunity for the youth,

Stop putting down the peasant. They too, need to be educated. Stop taking pride in knowing more than your neighbor. After all, a country where Voodoo is practiced, but where the Judeo-Christian culture has made big inroads, the command *"Love your neighbor just as yourself"* must be practiced.

We could institute a system of teaching the kids during the day and at night the kids would teach the adults.

4. **Eradicte corruption.** Stealing from the government is stealing from all of us. Send a delegation to Botswana to learn how to correct and continuously fight corruption. Education regarding corruption and economic crimes is badly needed. Corruption and impunity are considered as the twin evils causing Haiti's downfall. Haitians must monitor the assets and expenses of the politicians. We should follow what's required of the politicians regarding disclosing their assets on assuming a post in government and also on leaving. Transparence

in all aspects of governance will go a long way in bringing order in Haiti, where the Public Treasury is used as the piggy-bank of the powerful politicians who steal millions, then using impunity, they look in the face and say "If you can touch me."

A sort of brain washing campaign of the population is also in order. That was done effectively in Rwanda, following the internal genocide of 1994, to bring peace and reconciliation. Rwanda is now exemplary, not only for other African countries as a pillar of economic development.

We need role playing education of the kids. They need to understand what the other side is going through. They need to understand how much pain is caused when someone is shot, traumatized or killed. As the saying goes, "It takes a village!" It does take cooperation, because singlehandedly not much can be accomplished.

Educate, emphasizing "civic education." Education on trust. Use social media and traditional media to accomplish that.

Education will decrease inequality, a serious Haitian problem.

Health care education shouldn't be neglected.

Ask every Haitian to help in keeping the country clean, by just cleaning the front of their homes. To be applauded is the declaration of the new Prime Minister, who's launched a clean-up campaign of the Haitian capital.

Stop treating the diaspora as the enemy. Stop treating people that study outside as the enemy. There should be also a system to reintegrate that brain that comes with new ideas. The population should not be threatened by new knowledge. We should not chase them out of the country. We need them as much as the people that studied in the country. We are all in for the same cause.

5. We need an army of 50,000 to 80,000 soldiers, besides the police. That will also help the country's economy in a "Trickle Down Economics" aspect.

6. When the government gives a scholarship to one of us to go study abroad, there should be real incentives for us to come back.

7. Monitor banks whose tellers tip off their bandit friends about customers who just withdrew funds.

   Monitor the banks where people withdrawing funds have too often been held up.

8. If there's no 24/7 electricity, how will you deal with the new generation of "Hybrid or EV" cars? To be taken into account is that combustion cars will be a diminishing breed and more expensive, both to make and repair.

9. Democracy is not applicable in Haiti the way we know it. To start, the population needs to be educated to understand democracy. That will come after a period of rejuvenation.

10. Haiti will go nowhere, if our dear friend France stands too close by. Sometimes even a beloved family member can cause significant negative impacts, while attempting to help in our decision-making process. All the decisions and help from France so far, after 220 years of independence, have not worked for us. Haitians, if you keep making the same mistakes, you can't expect to obtain different results? *"Sispann anbrase franse a, pa kite l pwoche bò tete w, sèl fason pou l sispann mòde w!"*

11. A country's main industry cannot be kidnapping. People need to trust each other. The rule of law needs to be established in that part of the world. ***Reformatting Haitian's mentality*** is necessary. There should be severe penalties for crime perpetrators of all sorts. Punishment needs to be harsh to prevent recurrence and recidivism. If you have a notorious industry that is a breadwinner, but the bread is soaked in blood, don't expect it to disappear overnight, on its own. This must be addressed right now. **A delay will bring these terrible behaviors into Diasporaland and give Haitians abroad a very bad name also.** To the non-Haitians reading this book, if you think that cannot happen to your country, you are wrong, just as I was.

12. If you don't have any other profitable industry than tourism, your country must be safe. The richest European countries still rely on tourism. We should make sure it works for us also. Let me reiterate, if Port-au-Prince is on the list of the most dangerous cities in the world, you cannot expect to have much tourist activity. Annually, South Florida gets $13 billion in federal tax and $11 billion from state and local taxation on tourism. Haiti has great potential in that field. It's still a beautiful country, rich in historical sites, if properly developed and kept. Moreover, it is in close proximity to the powerhouse that is the United States of America. Very important indeed.

13. If your primary industry is agriculture, you must have roads and infrastructure. We need to redefine agriculture. It means that we need to replant the rice fields that are still vacant. We must make good use of fertilizers. We must use composting, and pasteurize human manure from the latrines.

Infrastructure projects should also include cleaning up the ravines and prevent construction, willy nilly, on the hillsides, that cause mudslides in rainy season, causing death and desolation.

Decongestion of the capital is very important.

14. No one will keep money in a country where people are afraid to use it. People need to feel free to spend their money. The country should be managed in such a way to attract investment. Liquidity will follow when peace is established. Then, the slogan *"Haiti is open for business"* won't sound hollow to foreign investors. The crooks belong in jail. If you are a capitalist country, you have to protect property. You cannot have people stealing land, even a small parcel of land, as if it were a piece of bread. Every wrong possession can't be treated like a Jean Valjean act. When I was growing up, stealing an egg was no less than stealing a cow. **The association of Notaries in Haiti should cancel the licenses of notaries that have been reported pending investigations. In Haiti the notary is the one recording the deeds of properties, stealing a property cannot be accomplished without the help of a notary.**

Haiti's National Archives, known as *"Archives Nationales d'Haïti"* was able to record documents going back to the 1800. Why can't *"Contributions,"* the government Tax Office, record the property deeds the same way?

15. You don't need to rely on your own currency, that is the *gourde*. Just use the US dollar. We don't need to pay to print it. There's no fear of counterfeit. When safety is established, the diaspora will bring a good amount of money to the country. If enough money comes in every month, you won't even need to have your own money. And you could use the money dedicated to print money for education.

Have you an idea how much money can be raised by every Haitian spending his or her social security monthly deposits in Haiti. It is working for the Dominican Republic and its diaspora. If we work together there's no limit as to where we can carry Haiti. **Nursing home businesses will flourish in Haiti if we are at peace.**

16. We are close to the United States and our GDP is very low. We could be a good source of competition for those Indian and Filipino telephone call centers. But telephone service and internet connections must be reliable. We need more English-speaking people. And I'll emphasize that you can't accomplish anything without electricity twenty-four hours a day. Do something to fix that. As I hinted earlier, the world is transitioning to EV. What will you do when it's fully implemented?

17. If you're counting on fishing to boost the economy, then fishing must be of a grade to be commercialized.

18. The government needs to be harsh on drug trafficking. Otherwise, the drug lords will become more powerful than those entrusted with law enforcement.

19. What happened to *"L'Union fait la Force"* (In Uunity there's Strength/) *E pluribus unum* (Out of many one people), mottos of Haiti? Haitians should be inspired by them. We need to defeat the distrust and strongly discourage deceiving practices. Stop blaming each other for the lack of success. We need to go after the strength within. Destroying everything when you are upset is only digging a bigger hole in which to be buried.

20. Uncontrolled use of fire should be illegal. We can't allow burning without restriction. It should be just for cooking or used in case smoke is needed for a task. We can't keep burning things that we cannot replace. We have been burning for more than 200 years. It has not taken us anywhere except for the independence. (stop the "Nap boule = we are burning). Prison time would be appropriate for people burning cars, houses, tires. It is not healthy for the population to keep breathing these toxic fumes. When they become sick later, it will be the responsibility of the government to care for them.

21. Decongestion of the capital could be part of the decentralization of Haiti., something of outmost necessity. You cannot be draining money burning gas in traffic as we do. Either the capital is moved to another location, or the streets have to be enlarged. The problem is that the people are too selfish to give a piece of land to enlarge the streets, and the government is not brave enough to enforce the rules and prevent people from taking part of the certain streets to supplement their front yard. We need to stop being so selfish and stop seizing parts of the streets. If the streets accommodate more cars, traffic will be smoother. The value of the houses will increase. Stress will diminish. Then a lot more will be accomplished in a day. A plus for everyone in the community.

22. If diplomacy works for most countries, it's doubtful that it will work well in Haiti, because the leadership lacks leverage in almost every way.

23. We must have respect for the dead. Most countries would not close a cemetery to turn it into a parking lot or a bus station. If someone is killed, why desecrate the remains by chopping up the body?

24. A great percentage of the population is made up of "undercover criminals." due to the fact that some businesses flourish in the present atmosphere. Thus, certain individuals abhor change. While they complain like everyone else, they are still happy with the money they get to take to the bank, from people who have no choice but to use their security company for protection. Of course, one who's selling security isn't keen at all on having peace. Consider a woman, whose husband is killing people to bring money home. She would pray every day for more people to be killed. Such a situation adds to the difficulty of fixing Haiti and introduce it on a better path. Consider this also. If you are selling imported rice, lime, corn, you're not enthusiastic about boosting the effort for locally grown products.

25. Clearly the Dominican Republic is profiting from Haiti's misfortune, with the leadership of that country not realizing that this could turn against them. Based on an unconfirmed report, the Dominicans were facilitating export of machine guns to Haiti, Now they've come up with a list of the bandits, who are outlawed in the Dominican Republic. However, the money extorted from the Haitian people is already pocketed by those same Dominicans. What will happen to the houses that the terrorists bought in the Dominican Republic? What will happen to the substantial amount of money they have deposited in Dominican Republic banks? Will the Dominican government confiscate both money and their houses? Will the money be turned over to the Haitian government? No issue is simple when it comes to Haiti!

26. Haunted by the question of Cubans still emigrating to Haiti while Haitians are leaving!

27. Try a different language. There must be a reason for the French language to be mandatory on the Colonization Tax agreement. Personally, I know several Americans who would be happy to go teach Haitians English for free.

28. There's much physical thinness in the diaspora because Haitian kids didn't get to visit Haiti. They have not formed a bond with cousins, brothers, sisters, or with the country itself. Please open up the country to increase the number of your sympathizers.

    Whatever you do to make Haiti a better place now for your kids is better than the financial heritage you're leaving them. The earlier the country is open, the better it will be for all parties involved.

29. We need to work arduously on the problem of deforestation., first, by decreasing the use of charcoal for cooking. And a campaign to plant trees must be undertaken, initially by hand on the sides of

the mountains, then via seeding by airplanes. The erosion of the Haitian soil is reaching a dreadful level.

29b. *"Jamais dodo"* (Never sleep) call center comes to the fore, because there's always someone awake somewhere. In that light, contacting other countries about projects that have the potential to make a positive impact is encouraged. Haiti needs to continuously be looking for private investments from all over the world. There are a lot of megarich people looking to invest somewhere. We need to be a secure place and they have to be guaranteed a good return on investment.

30. Every single paper any Haitian politician sign should be published in *"Le Moniteur,"* the State's official gazette, within a deadline. Politicians cannot keep signing papers for the country without our knowledge. If they are or were not published and approved by our legal process they are null and void.

31. We need potable water to decrease the dissemination of diseases.

32. STOP BEGGING. You will only get 17 motos anyway. Respect yourself and us too.

33. **Human rights cannot be one-sided.** There can't be democracy if there is no education to help understand what it is.

If your behavior is not appropriate, no matter how much someone needs you, he/she will have no respect for you.

Haiti, wake up! We need to trust each other. We need to work well with each other. We need to give back to the country. Let the roots of Toussaint Louverture grow. You can kill us but the tree will grow back, because its roots are deep and alive. Go ahead, kill me. Go ahead, make martyr of me.

34. The same way that KPK = *Kanal la Pap Kanpe*, *BPK = Batay la Pap Kampe!* There's no way to stop the campaign to make of Haiti what it's meant to be from its early beginning: *The Pearl of the Antilles!*

    Haiti could use some new blood. San Salvador sounds like one of the secrets. San Salvador is the magic bullet for Haiti's last misfortune.

35. We do what we do best. Have parties to raise money for the first paycheck for the new army. Have parties in NY, NJ, CT, calling on all volunteers, musicians also volunteering. This is just a message that we are sending. Just a message.

36. The government must increase revenue, not for the salaries of more Secretaries of State appointed, but for more development programs. It is well known that Haitians do not pay tax. They are going to look for any excuse not to pay tax. Therefore, the government must get the tax via the surest way possible. Forget about the traditional taxable items. Tax more fuel. Tax more stuff that you can monitor, or they cannot cheat on and reduce the tax on things they will tend to get away with without paying taxes.

37. Make a deal with a big car manufacturer, give it monopoly of a limited number of years to import cars in Haiti, they built the roads, the government add a surcharge on other imported cars.

38. Any entity of the government that deals with money must be audited every year and the auditors scrutinized

The country has paid more than its dues, leave us alone.

THE LAST WORD

The country is not cursed, and it has paid more than its dues. Enough of the senseless killings. The consensus in the Haitian community is that no one cares about us. Haiti did not exist before Ukraine or Gaza and Haiti will still be inexistant during and after the reconstruction of those places.

Funny that human rights were born and started in Haiti and Haitians cannot enjoy those rights. civil rights as we know them in the western world cannot be applied in Haiti. Civil rights are difficult to administer in complete and total anarchy and poverty not alone ignorance. There is no love, no spirit of belonging, no trust, no joy. Moral is low, there is lost faith. Haitians have given up. I hope it doesn't last this time around.

Haiti, El Salvador did it and Haiti is behind you. The powers that be are rightfully promoting human rights. Based on the number of Haitians I spoke to, I can assure the world that more than 80% would rather have a dictatorship than the type of human rights that is offered to them right now. The understandable exceptions would be family members of people that the Duvalier regime and others killed. The world needs to worry because Haiti is pioneer in a lot of things. Haiti's situation is coming to a theater near you. Mark my words.

My role is to make sure you know how Haiti's future was robbed. My job is to tell you where the money is. I have even told you how to collect. What you do with that information is up to you.

There is no real reason why El Salvador could not be helping us out. As usual, future will tell how much help we are getting now. Meanwhile, our exodus continues to overseas or over to heaven since the population is already in hell.

In reality, nothing I can think, say or do will change Haiti unless the outside world is stopped in interfering in Haiti's business, or the Haitians take complete control of their fate no matter where it takes them. Stop being the puppets on the string.

After spending so much time and energy explaining the horrible things that are happening and have been happening in Haiti. I must tell you that there is no word in reality to do this tragedy justice.

END

GGTLM

THE PAINTINGS IN THIS BOOK ARE THE PROPERTY OF HAITIAN HOLOKAUSTON MUSEUM

GERARD GERMAIN, M.D.

EDUCATIONAL AND PROFESSIONAL TRAINING

January 1982 - December 1986	Universidad Del Noreste 6315 Av. Hidalgo Tampico TAM, Mexico M.D. Degree.
October 1987 - June 1988	Fifth Pathway Program - Rotating Clinical Clerkship Cabrini Medical Center, New York, New York/New York Medical College, Valhalla, New York
July 1988 - June 1991	Internship/Residency St. Joseph's Medical Center Family Practice Residency Program Yonkers, New York
July 1990 - June 1991	Chief Resident St. Joseph's Medical Center Family Practice Residency Program Yonkers, New York
July 1991 - April 1992	Attending Physician in Geriatric St. Joseph's Medical Center.
April 1992 July 1993	Faculty of the Family Practice Residency Program
April 1992 - July 1993	Director of School Health Program in Yonkers New York
July 1991 - To present	Emergency Room Physician
May 1993 2002	Co-editor, St. Joseph's Medical Center Family Practice Residency Program Newsletter
Sept 1995 1999	Saint Joseph's Medical Center Emergency Department Q.A. Coordinator.

Oct 1988 2000	Volunteer, The New York City Marathon 23 miles Medical team.
Oct 1997 1999	American Academy of Family Physician Bronx/Westchester Chapter Public Health Committee Chairman.
Sept 2001 2006	Lecturer, Physician Assistant Program Mercy College Dobbs Ferry, New York.
2019	Lecturer Forrest General Family Practice Residency program
2016	William Carey University College of Osteopathic Medicine Adjunct Professor
2019	Motivational speaker

BOOKS AND PUBLICATIONS

The Funny Bunch, children's book
Valentine's Day
Rape Is Real, The Truth Revealed
G's Medical Study Guide
A Walk Down Medicine Memory Lane
Documentation At Its Best, Vital But Underused
Tool In Medical Practice
The Luckiest Man Who Grew Up In An Engineered
and Manufactured Poverty. In English, Spanish,
Italian, French and Creole. Featured in the New York
Times. 09/29/2020
Eiffel Tower, Pride Of Haiti. In English, Spanish,
French and Creole

HONORS AND AWARDS

American Academy of Family Physicians,
Award for Excellence in Patient Education, 1990

Arnold A. Migliaccio, M.D. Award for Overall
Academic Achievement and Excellence on surgical
Rotation, 1991

1997 Family Practice Award for continuing contribution to the Saint Joseph's Family Practice Residency Program.

Emergency Cardiac Care Award
American Heart Association
for initiating ECC Successfully in Central Park, New York

MEMBERSHIP/CERTIFICATIONS

American Academy of Family Physicians

New York Academy of Family Physicians

Mississippi Academy of Family Physicians

Certified in Hypnotism New York City

RESEARCH/ PUBLICATIONS

Prediction of (CHF) Congestive Heart Failure by Changes on Signal Averaging.

Patient Compliance and Reversal of Disease on Zero Cholesterol Diet.

Study of diflucan/ Fluconazole use

LANGUAGES

Fluent in Creole, French, English, Spanish.

Poems Written:
- My therapy group.
- California.
- Voyage to the infinite.
- Vacation.
- Return to paradise.
- Love is closer than you think.

Songs Written:
- California.
- America, I love you.
- Just believe in yourself.

- Motel California.
- Heckation (Vacation)

Books involved in:
Rape Is Real The Truth Revealed.
The Funny Bunch

Articles written:

- Alternating Tylenol and Motrin to control fever in babies while decreasing the potential complication of either medications 1992.
- Preventing medical disaster by monitoring blood thinners.
- Preventing Zika infection and mosquito bite by taking vitamin B1.
- CPR band
- Poppy seeds as cause of positive drug screening.
- Fire Prevention.
- The trill sign.
- A case of situs inversus.
- Pacemaker for the brain.
- Alternative treatment for osteoarthritis. With synvisc.
- OTC Antibiotic?
- Toradol, new tool for pain management.
- Lyme disease.
- Child safety.
- Germain maneuver.

- Radyo Independence on Facebook and 90.9 FM New York October 2nd, 2021, with Jacques Dorville.
- WSRF 1580 AM 06/28/2021
- Radio Haiti America International, Clark Jacques and Andre Fouad WSRF 1580 am / W25HCZ 92.5 fm 06/21/2021
- Haiti premiere classe, Theodore Fayette 06/13/2021
- Afrikreyol Lady Na 05/27/2021
- on line with Pasteur Matthieu Delisme 04/2020
- NY Times book section 03/29/2020
- Radio Television Haitiana RTHaitiana.com 03/2020
- Island TV, Patrick Eliancy 03/2020
- Radio Haiti publicite, Ronald Coltaire 01/2020
- WDAM National TV Channel 7 Mississippi 02/2020
- WHPM Fox 23 TV Mississippi
- Anacaona TV 02/2020

- Ronald Leon Show 02/2020
- Radio Fierte Haitienne 02/2020

Other media appearances.
- Radio Soleil
- Pyrotechnic TV New York
- Heat stroke TV Mississippi
- Zika TV Mississippi
- AIDS Radio Florida.
- Myocardial infarction (Heart attack) Radio Florida.

Inventions:
- EKG pads.
- Nail clipper with nail collector.
- Lighted Intubation stylet.
- Central line insertion kit.
- Female Voiding Apparatus.

Printed in the USA
CPSIA information can be obtained
at www.ICGtesting.com
LVHW021157110924
790748LV00003B/18

9 798894 192277